Praise for *The Power of Ownership*

"This book is a fantastic blend of science and practical application to help you have the energy to power your ambitions. Something like this can ONLY be written by someone who's on the field every day, helping people master their stamina, health, and wellness. I love it when practitioners, instead of researchers and regurgitators, write books. If you want to stay average, don't read this book."

—**Todd Herman,**
Author of *The Alter Ego Effect*, Coach, Entrepreneur

"A must-read for anyone currently a leader. Having experienced the toll of stress and burnout, I'm grateful for Justin's book, which teaches you how to live life by design. It's a roadmap to personalized health, helping you understand what might be healthy for others but harmful to you. It is the next level of Atomic Habits."

—**Tom Patterson,**
Founder and CEO of Tommy John

"Justin does a marvelous job of showing the reader exactly how to 'OWN' their life and live a life by design—taking control and having a plan for how to live the best life possible. Justin's passion oozes out of the pages and really leaves the reader with a bulletproof game plan of action moving forward!"

—**David Nurse,**
Wall Street Journal Bestselling Author, Top 50 Worldwide Keynote Speaker, Mindset and Mental Skills Specialist

"There's a reason why inflight announcements remind you to secure your own oxygen mask before helping others. Justin's work is a nice reminder that for us to be of service to others, we need to be the best version of ourselves first. You can't pour from an empty cup, and Justin provides practical solutions to ensure your cup begins to overflow!"

—**Art Horne,**
VP of performance Boston Celtics NBA

"There are few on the planet more passionate and articulate when it comes to optimizing health and performance than Justin. His energy spills out of the pages as he educates, motivates, inspires, and empowers all of us to be champions, and live life by design."

—Teena Murray,
High Performance Thought Leader, and NBA and NHL Executive

"Justin Roethlingshoefer is one of the powerhouses in the health, fitness, and peak personal performance space. His combination of education, real-world experience, and vision to change the world makes him one of the modern-day gurus in life-coaching and performance. His mission, vision, and desire to impact the world is inspiring. Do yourself a big favor and read *The Power of Ownership*. It will undoubtedly help every aspect of your physical health and energy as well as your mindset, soulset, and heartset."

—Todd Durkin, M.A., CSCS,
Two-Time Trainer of the Year and Jack LaLanne Award Recipient,
Bestselling Author of *Get Your Mind Right*, Founder,
IMPACT-X Performance Coaching

"Justin, a true expert in the field of sleep and performance, brings unparalleled knowledge and insight to the forefront. Justin's expertise is a beacon of wisdom in the realm of performance science, making him a go-to source for anyone striving to unlock their full potential."

—Todd Anderson,
Sleep Expert, Founder of Dream Recovery

"If you are overly stressed, facing personal or professional challenges, living in default mode, struggling with your health, or just looking for tools to feel and perform your best, *The Power of Ownership* is for you! Justin Roethlingshoefer has spent decades helping the best athletes and business leaders reclaim their health and live a purpose-driven life. He is now bringing these same tools to the rest of us in a transformative and authentic guide to reclaiming control of your health and life. This book should be self-assigned reading for anyone looking for a roadmap to a more fulfilling life."

—Juliet Starrett,
New York Times Bestselling author of *Built to Move*

"Justin is hands-down one of the biggest thought leaders when it comes to health and energy optimization for business and industry leaders. He influences the influencer, and leads the leader. His combination of art, science, and real-life application makes his principles the most holistic and actionable in the industry. Being involved in OWN IT since inception, the company has perfected the individualization model to where it has been able to impact not only me but my entire corporation, the fastest-growing real estate group in the world. Everything he and his team do is in this resource, and it is a no-brainer to have this as mandatory reading for anyone in leadership and your team."

—Sharran Srivatsaa,
President REAL Brokerage

"This isn't just a book; it's a transformative roadmap for those yearning for a profound shift in health and performance. Justin's empowering book democratizes the wisdom you need to reclaim your health and take ownership of your own journey. With a focus on personalized lifestyle design, it empowers you to break free from what is considered normal, offering a path to live differently and shape a reality aligned with your unique choices."

—Amberly Lago,
Bestselling Author, Top 1% Podcast Host, Peak Performance Coach

"*The Power of Ownership* is an extraordinary, complete and robust tool that empowers the reader to stop living a default life and instead begin to curate a life by design. We all deserve to achieve our highest and greatest potential; unfortunately, for many, they don't know where to start. Justin makes it not only easy to understand but makes you want to start today."

—Rudi Riekstins,
Top 5 Business Coach

"In *The Power of Ownership: Redeem Your Health, Live Life by Design,* Justin Roethlingshoefer channels raw intensity and unmatched expertise from years of guiding top athletes, bringing to life a revolutionary approach to holistic health. Having witnessed firsthand the peril of neglecting one's health, Justin is on a fervent mission—not just for athletes, but for every leader hungry for success. Dive deep beyond the conventional. Justin challenges the 'Myth of Normal,' revealing how society's acceptance of stress and fatigue has clouded our perceptions. With his book, you not only receive a master class in reclaiming your vitality, but you're also empowered with tangible strategies to maintain it. He crafts a dynamic blend of artistry with avant-garde health science—shunning generic solutions in favor of personalized blueprints. This isn't just another read. It's a movement—an invigorating exploration of living authentically, attuned to the unique needs of your body and mind. For anyone ready to defy the status quo and truly own their health, *The Power of Ownership* will redefine your journey and reignite passion within your team. Trust me, I've worked with Justin and stand behind everything he teaches."

—Adam Jablin,
Creator and Founder of THE HERO PROJECT

"I am forever grateful for the positive effects Justin has brought into my life. He is an individual who has walked through the valleys that life can throw your way. With his positive mindset, an unconquerable spirit, and a brilliant mind; he is on a quest to redeem the health of the world. Through his life's work and *The Power of Ownership*, he combines research, science, and real-life application into one of the best resources I have ever seen. Those whom I serve are now served at a higher level because I can now show up with greater capacity to be the best version of myself possible, and in turn, the ripple effect begins. This is not just a book, but a resource that will change your health, energy, and understanding of how to build habits that mean something to you. This is a can't-miss if you are looking to elevate the way you look, feel, and live."

—Elisa Angeles,
Assistant Athletic Director and Director of Sports
Performance Florida State University

"Justin's unwavering commitment to health and performance positions him as a dynamic leader in the field. Dive into this transformative book if you're ready to transcend theory and embrace actionable steps that make real wisdom that is different from any resource you have used in the past available at your fingertips. This is not just about learning; it's a guide to hands-on practices tailored to your individual needs, empowering you to cultivate a resilient body and a revitalized sense of ownership over your health."

—Kevin Rutherfod,
CEO Culture First Leadership and Board Member
Nestlé Health Science Company

"Justin has democratized true health and high performance. He has made everything that is available to the best athletes and elites in the world available to everyone in this book. Being able to speak firsthand to the experience with Justin and The OWN IT team is like something I haven't even encountered even at the NHL level. It's different. When you lean in, your health changes and so does your life."

—Anders Lee,
Captain of the New York Islanders (NHL)

JUSTIN
ROETHLINGSHOEFER

THE
POWER
OF
OWNERSHIP

REDEEM YOUR HEALTH,
LIVE LIFE BY DESIGN, AND
**BREAK THE RELENTLESS
PURSUIT OF NORMAL**

FOREWORD BY **DAVID MELTZER**

WILEY

Published by John Wiley & Sons, Inc., Hoboken, New Jersey.
Published simultaneously in Canada.

For general information on our other products and services or for technical support, please contact our Customer Care Department within the United States at (800) 762-2974, outside the United States at (317) 572-3993 or fax (317) 572-4002.

Wiley also publishes its books in a variety of electronic formats. Some content that appears in print may not be available in electronic formats. For more information about Wiley products, visit our web site at www.wiley.com.

Library of Congress Cataloging-in-Publication Data:

Names: Roethlingshoefer, Justin, author.
Title: The power of ownership : redeem your health, live life by design,
   and break the relentless pursuit of normal / Justin Roethlingshoefer.
Description: First edition. | Hoboken, New Jersey : Wiley, [2024] |
   Includes index.
Identifiers: LCCN 2023055135 (print) | LCCN 2023055136 (ebook) | ISBN
   9781394230020 (hardback) | ISBN 9781394230044 (adobe pdf) | ISBN
   9781394230037 (epub)
Subjects: LCSH: Self-care, Health. | Self-actualization (Psychology)
Classification: LCC RA776.95 .R64 2024 (print) | LCC RA776.95 (ebook) |
   DDC 613—dc23/eng/20240104
LC record available at https://lccn.loc.gov/2023055135
LC ebook record available at https://lccn.loc.gov/2023055136

Cover Design: Wiley
Cover Image: © gonin/Getty Images
Author Photo: Courtesy of the Author
SKY10068649_030524

Contents

Foreword

I DEFINE JOY as the consistent (meaning every day), persistent (meaning without quit), pursuit of your potential. When it comes to our well-being, consistency is key. As I read Justin's profound words in *The Power of Ownership*, I'm reminded of the incredible power of consistency and intentionality to form positive habits and propel us on the trajectory of where we are called to and higher. This book is a testament to the transformative capacity of taking ownership for our own journey, and it's my privilege to introduce you to a roadmap that will empower you to take back control of your health and change your life, while allowing you to truly enjoy the pursuit of your potential.

It also is important to understand that the seasons of our life are certain to change and evolve over time. I became a multimillionaire just two years out of law school, I married my dream girl, and it looked like I had everything I wanted. But the people who loved me warned me about the path I was on. As Justin will dive into, I was living a life by default.

I was engaging in unhealthy habits that were holding me back from giving my best to myself, my family, and my friends, not to mention putting me on the fast track to illness and sickness. Their warnings led to my eventual realization that I needed to do something different if I wanted to realize the life and longevity that I deeply desired. That set me on a journey that led to an overwhelming sense of gratitude, and you are about to embark on that same journey, and have it spelled out to you in a personalized way. It was not an easy road taking ownership of my life. I've faced battles, setbacks, and moments when my health was at stake. The struggle is real, but so is the potential for transformation. That is why it's worth it.

Justin's message is clear: you don't have to settle for what the world tells you is normal. You don't have to accept the common results. You can live differently, as I have, as Justin has, and as countless others you look up to have. We live in a world that often pushes us toward dysfunctional patterns in pursuit of success. The struggles are familiar—body image issues, addiction, burnout, and more—but there is hope, and it starts with a decision to be different. The decision to live differently and live a life by design.

Justin has dedicated his life to the purpose of redeeming the health of the world, and *The Power of Ownership* exemplifies that commitment. He distills decades of experience and education, both personal and professional, into a clear and actionable guide for taking control of your health and your life. This is not a one-size-fits-all approach. Instead, it's a toolkit that empowers you to understand your body, your unique needs, and your path to holistic health, wellness, and performance.

As you read these pages, you'll develop a newfound understanding of your body and the skills, knowledge, and desire to make intentional change. You'll walk away with a personalized action plan and the resources you need to make your journey sustainable and purposeful. This book is more than words on pages; it's a promise and a path to living a more fulfilling life by design. A true collision of science and application. Only you have the power to change your own life, and by the end of this book, Justin will have shown you how. It is my pleasure to welcome you to *The Power of Ownership*.

David Meltzer

Introduction

I ROLLED OVER in my bed and kissed my wife on her cheek as I do every morning before I spring out of bed. As I put my shorts and T-shirt on and walked outside to take my morning picture of the sunrise (#wakeupthesun), I had an overwhelming feeling of gratitude. The energy, alertness, and deep feeling of holistic wellness that I embodied was not something that I always had. It was a battle, a journey, and a learning experience that nearly cost me my life. As a young boy, my father said something to me that caused me to think differently from the age of 12. He said, "Son, talent will get you noticed, but consistency will get you paid." It was then that I knew I wanted to be the most consistent version of myself, and it started with my daily habits. That was Day 1 of ownership.

Just like you, I have decided to live a certain way that has generated a certain life; however, some of you are not pleased with your results. That is why I have to help you live differently. There have been many iterations of this over my life, but for the first time I can honestly say that I know what true health feels like. Mental, physical, spiritual, and emotional health, all in rhythm, engaging in a beautiful dance through an intertwining web of art, science, and design. A life by design, and now so can you.

I didn't always know what a life done differently looked like, or felt like. I was caught in the dichotomy of knowing I wanted to feel and live differently, but fell into the dysfunctional patterns that the world of athletics, entrepreneurship, and success tell us are normal. I struggled with:

- Body image issues
- Anorexia
- Addiction
- Burnout
- Sleeplessness
- Body pains
- Brain fog
- Chronic illness
- Fatigue
- Overwhelm
- A fear I wasn't doing enough
- A desire to "keep up"

When I set out to write *The Power of Ownership*, I rewrote the outline 15 times and rewrote the book 6 times before being able to settle on it. I remember sitting with *New York*

Times best-selling author and speaker Jon Gordon, as he encouraged me to really lean into this book. We were driving to the airport after he crushed me at pickleball in Jacksonville, Florida, and he said, "This is the book you have to write. If you own your health, you can own your life. And you have the formula to do it." After sending him the first outline, he sent back an email saying, "You have three different books here. This is a common issue with writers where they will try to fit everything into one book."

Getting clarity and simplifying what is on these pages is the same thing that plagues you in your health journey. You try to do everything, all at once, not understanding what you need, and you actually end up doing nothing. You try to emulate someone else, instead of understanding your body and knowing that you may need to do something different and being okay with that. You get overwhelmed, confused, and frustrated, often giving up before you even give yourself a chance to realize results.

As I crossed the last 't' and dotted the last *i* on this book I knew every experience I have had personally, but also helping the best athletes and business leaders redeem their health and live a life by design, set me up to write this book. The best athletes and business leaders are no different than you; they have simply chosen to live differently, and it has rewarded them with different levels of energy, mental clarity, focus, and drive. Some began doing it at 20 years old and some at 60 years old, so no matter where you are today, the great news is it's never too late, and it starts with a decision to be different. My goal is to give you back your power and authority so you can take ownership of the journey to redeeming your health, live your life by design, and realize results that are different.

Reach, Teach, Empower

This book is meant to *reach* and speak to you. Something you can relate to. To *teach* and educate you in a way that is not about more information but rather about generating an understanding and awareness about your body and how you can live a life by design that has not been available before. Last, this book is meant to *empower* you. A tool that will for the first time provide a framework for you to take ownership of your health in a holistically integrated and personalized way. A manual that you will continue to refer back to and use to design your life.

You won't get the robotic and cookie-cutter approach that should work for "everyone" in this book. Instead, you will get the tools, systems, and processes to generate your life by design, to take ownership of your health. The same systems and processes I developed working at the highest level of sport with the best athletes, entrepreneurs, and leaders in the world. You will develop confidence in yourself, knowing that you understand your body in a way that did not make sense before.

I take great responsibility in that. It is not about putting more information out into the world, or exposing my voice, but ensuring that through this book a relationship is built, responsibility is taken, and influence is generated, to begin to redeem the health of the world, starting with you, which I was called to do more than two decades years ago.

I am sure you have read all the other habit, health, and personal development books that tell you what you should be engaging in, but there are two major flaws in this process.

- It provides information without an application. Meaning that you cannot fully understand it.

- Advice is very context dependent. Even though something worked in the author or creator's life doesn't mean it will work in yours.

In fact, what the world tells us is healthy may actually be killing you. In this book I won't tell you *what* to do, but rather outline a system that empowers you on *how* to do it, eliminating the confusion and overwhelm once and for all. This is the inverse of the way culture tells you to do it.

I want you to get really good at asking yourself better questions. This is going to bring you heightened awareness that will lead to better decision-making and create exponential growth in your health. I want you to ponder and carry around certain questions without generating an immediate response. Questions like:

- What am I optimizing for?
- Where in my health am I wanting to see the change?
- What impact are my current habits and behaviors having on my health and how am I measuring that?
- Are my current habits going to get me to where I want to be?
- What does my calendar tell me about my priorities?
- What do my current behaviors tell me about my priorities?
- Are my current instincts empowering me to live abundantly?

You will find questions in this book over advice, and a system over a set of rules. Where questions are able to help you generate clarity and context that will make this journey very personal as you develop ownership. My prayer is that as you read you will have repeated wake-up calls and paradigm shifts that leave you with a new understanding of your body and how to take ownership of your health.

My Promise

What I promise you is that you will get the following in this book:

- **My heart, knowledge, and experience:** God gave me a heart for people. I am someone who knew their purpose since they were 12 years old and pursued it relentlessly with conviction. It empowered my vision: to redeem the health of the world. It led to opportunities to study at some of the greatest institutions, with some of the most brilliant minds that helped to create a philosophy that heals. It provided experiences to be around some of the most successful business people and athletes and learn how to apply the philosophies in a system that works. Not just once, but repeatedly.

    God has also given me the resilience to handle the mountain tops and the valleys, to work at the highest level of sport, to be responsible for some of the best athletes in the world and most successful business owners, and realize that we were not solving an athlete problem but a *human problem*.

- **Simplicity and relatability:** This is not a textbook and it is not a storybook. It is a manual. It is the unique intersection point of art and science that you will be able to understand, relate to, and apply to your life immediately.

- **An actionable tool:** By the end of this book, you will have had a paradigm shift in how you see your health holistically, and a new understanding for the body that you inhabit. You will also have an action plan and several resources to make your journey sustainable and purposeful that are designed for you.

- **My presence:** I mentioned this is not just a book with a bunch of information, but a tool that I want to impact for generations to come. To change the way you and your entire family approach your health. This was not written on a whim or in between meetings and phone calls. I put my ultimate presence into this, stepping away from business, keynotes, and workshops to ensure it was exactly what it was supposed to be.

When you live a life by design, you are able to identify your formula to win abundantly. Not just once but repeatedly; not just in one bucket of life either, but holistically. It becomes a formula that allows you to live differently than everyone else and get results that are not available to everyone else, thus making you different. When you live differently, life looks different.

When I built my company and wrote *The Power of Ownership*, I wanted to give people an experience in the domain of health and wellness that was different from anything else they could get anywhere. That is what you are about to step into today. An experience that will require self-reflection and a different perspective than you have approached health and life with before. It will challenge you, but it will take you out of what you thought was normal. It will bless you with new understanding and allow you to live life differently and by design. Welcome to *The Power of Ownership*.

PART

I

Understanding Different

1

From Normal to Different

"What is normal? Normal is only ordinary; mediocre. Life belongs to the rare, exceptional individual who dares to be different."
—V.C. Andrews

ACCORDING TO MERRIAM-WEBSTER, the word *normal* is defined as "conforming to a type, standard, or regular pattern: characterized by that which is considered usual, typical, or routine."

What does *normal* mean? I'm not talking about the definition, but rather the reality. What does the world tell us *normal* is?

- It's normal to work to the point of exhaustion.
- It's normal to lack consistency.
- It's normal to lose control of your body when you get married and have kids.

3

- It's normal to gain weight after you leave college and start your career.
- It's normal to have your mind race at night and not be able to sleep.
- It's normal to have brain fog and walk into a room while completely forgetting why you went in there.
- It's normal to have a beer or a glass of wine every night to wind down.
- It's normal to be overwhelmed with worry and anxiety.
- It's normal to wake up with no energy to power you through your day.
- It's normal to live like everyone else around you because you are too busy to learn about your body.

These dysfunctional norms are how the world has trained you to be average, and how it has convinced you that health is the absence of disease. I'm here to tell you it's all a lie. True health is thriving physically, mentally, emotionally, and spiritually.

Debunking the Myth That "Normal" Is "Healthy"

Aristotle said, "We are what we repeatedly do. Excellence, then, is not an act but a habit." Your choices, behaviors, and life experiences give you the ability to predict outcomes. You logically know what will happen next. You feel in control. At the flip of a light switch, you know the light will illuminate. When you turn on the faucet, there will be water. When you turn the key in the ignition, the car will start.

It's an extremely rare and unbelievable experience when "what you know to be true" is now out of your control. The power is out. The water main was shut off. The engine won't turn over. Simple conveniences have been interrupted. What you know is the truth has now been left in doubt. What you engaged in daily was taken for granted. You unconsciously went from repeatedly doing something with intentionality to simply completing actions, the opposite of excellence.

What if your health was interrupted in the same way?

I had just come out of the procedure. Still groggy and "not all with it," I remember asking, "How did it go?" For the first time in almost a year the pain in my stomach was indistinguishable, but I didn't know if that was due to what I just went through or the anesthesia.

Coming into this day I had been the picture of health on the outside. Clean, organic diet; physically fit; minimal but purposeful supplements; made sure I was always hydrated; and made my physical health a priority. What was forgotten however was everything else. The other 75% of health. The mental, emotional, and spiritual side of things and how they relate to stress.

As an aspiring performance coach in the National Hockey League (NHL), and an entrepreneur with a young business, I was constantly on the road, eating at restaurants, sleeping in different beds at odd hours, away from family and loved ones for long periods of time. I regularly found myself under copious amounts of stress that I was never taught to deal with, and as a leader, I felt compelled to have all the answers, all while trying to do it on my own. After a decade of this pace being my version of normal, I had started to get these pains and heavy bloating in my stomach, but every doctor, specialist, and functional practitioner said all the tests revealed I was perfectly healthy, but they still offered to put me on testosterone therapy and various supplements to solve my problems. I knew that was not the solution and something was wrong.

It had gotten so bad that my diet consisted of smoothies and soup. I was losing weight, my energy was a fraction of what it had used to be, and I could not sleep. I had known it for a while but didn't want to admit it. My lifestyle, habits, and the inability to protect the temple in which I was currently inhabiting were all leading me to earn whatever chronic illness was brewing inside.

After two years of living with this pain, the final straw hit. I was in Chicago with my wife, Alyse, and we were working out in the hotel gym. Halfway through the workout I felt everything pause and the room slowly got dark. Down I went, head bouncing off the floor as my body followed shortly behind. Alyse gathered me up, walked me to our room, and sat me down. With a goose egg on my head and blurred vision, I saw a deeply concerned look on her face and remember her saying, "We need to get this figured out. This is not okay, and I need you here."

A "healthy" young man in his late 20s should not be feeling this way, yet everyone told me I was the picture of health and that this was normal for the stress I was under, and that stress was normal when building the career I wanted to build. However, I knew there was more to it.

After many phone consultations and specialist visits, there was finally a doctor in New York City who was willing to do an endoscopy and colonoscopy on this athletic and fit male in his late 20s. This brings us back to the post-procedure room.

"How did it go?" I asked.

"Well, I am so sorry that it took you so long to get to this point. If we had waited any longer, I am not sure you would have made it to your 35th birthday."

They had found four polyps the size of my thumb, all precancerous, along with a quarter-sized ulcer at the top of my stomach, also precancerous.

"We got everything. You have a new chance to live differently."

Reflecting back on it only makes the passion for my mission burn stronger. I had earned what had occurred. I had been investing in what the world told me was "normal" and in all the "things" I was told I needed, but failed at the fundamentals and what mattered to me. I had red-light beds, was regularly in the sauna and cold plunge, had all the meditation gadgets, and would get IVs once a month, but I forgot about my sleep, stress, and what my body was actually asking for.

The years of chronic stress, worry, undisciplined late nights, sporadic alcohol-laden events, spiritual disconnect, and inability to boundary time just for me had led to what would have been a death sentence and premature exit from this world. It is the "normal" way you are likely going through life, and you are likely being bombarded with companies telling you they have a quick fix, but I am here to tell you it is only masking what is not working.

I was recently talking with a pastor of a well-known super church, and he said, "Justin, I have done five funerals this quarter, all of them men and women under 60 years old. All of them were business leaders. All from chronic illness." The potential, the callings, the giftings, and the impact that have been left unfulfilled because of our inability to understand and manage our bodies is devastating.

That would have been me. Thirty-five, at best, if I had not figured out that what the world was telling me was healthy and normal was, in fact, killing me. Even as I was developing frameworks and systems for the best athletes in the world to live a life by design, and mitigate injury and illness to optimize health and performance, I had failed to be able to do it for myself. However, God saved me so that I could empower, guide, and encourage you to live differently.

Some Sobering Statistics about "Normal"

One recent statistic is that 70% of C-suite executives, entrepreneurs, and business leaders are looking at quitting their jobs for their well-being due to chronic health issues and burnout. Forgoing their mission because it has cost them their health.[1] The dysfunction they chose to live in finally caught up with them because everyone around told them it was normal.

I often hear the argument that modern medicine is ineffective, and many of you may not like this next statement. The problem isn't the medical system. The system was built to be reactive and make money, and by those standards, it is extremely effective. In fact, there have been extraordinarily large amounts of resources, knowledge, and effort put toward becoming the best reactive system in the world, and it has worked. The problem is that there has not been a system focused on the prevention of illness, and that you and I are more than willing to give away our power and authority when it comes to our health, habits, and lifestyles rather than to take ownership. Ignorance causes unnecessary suffering, and I no longer want you to suffer.

Prevention is better than a cure, but prevention requires you to have a system that educates and empowers you to be a champion for your own health. So you can know the truth and take a stand. It can no longer be acceptable to live in a state of confusion around your health, unable to take ownership for your decisions. It would be like driving down a highway at 100 miles per hour, and instead of taking a left or right at the fork in the road, slamming into the median because you didn't plan ahead or pick a direction to go in.

The current health trends speak volumes for what our current norm is causing:

- 77% of people experience stress that affects their physical health and 73% of people suffer from stress that impacts their mental health.[2]
- Someone dies every 33 seconds from cardiovascular disease, while someone else has a heart attack every 40 seconds.[3]
- Heart disease is the leading cause of death for men and women,[4] increasing at a rate of 50% over the past 30 years.[5]
- Two-thirds of adults are overweight or obese (69%) and one out of three are obese (36%). At this rate, by 2030, estimates predict that roughly half of all men and women will be obese,[6] increasing at a rate of 170% in the last 30 years.[7]
- 60% of adults in the United States have chronic illness, 40% of adults have two or more forms (diabetes, heart disease, cancer, chronic lung disease, stroke, Alzheimer's/type 3 diabetes, chronic kidney disease) that have been caused by lifestyle factors.[8]

- More than 37 million U.S. adults have diabetes, which is a 120% increase over the last 30 years, and 1 in 5 of them don't know they have it. In the last 20 years, the number of adults diagnosed with diabetes has more than doubled, while being the leading cause of kidney failure.[9]
- Type 2 diabetes rates rise at an alarming rate,[10] and the inability to process insulin is the fuel that increases type 3 diabetes or otherwise known as Alzheimer's disease.[11]
- 5.8 million people suffer from Alzheimer's and that number doubles every 5 years beyond age 65 and is expected to triple to 60 million by 2060.[12]
- 60% of people described their average, daily lives as "hectic."[13]
- Depression rates have increased 50% since 1990.[14]
- Suicide mortality rates have increased 37% since 2001 with a slight decline from 2018 to 2020, but have since returned to their peak.[15]
- Death rates from cancer have hardly moved over the last 50 years, and we are seeing for the first time in the history of the world a three-year decline in average lifespan of both men and women.[16]
- Less than 3% of Americans have a healthy lifestyle.[17]

These numbers individually are disturbing, but it's the fact we have normalized them that really moves me. It is said that more than 60% of premature deaths are preventable by habit and lifestyle change.[18] A lack of knowledge and understanding will cause you to perish, especially when you reject the truth. It is time to accept the truth as something different, and that is a life by design.

A New Perspective on "Different"

Merriam-Webster defines *different* as "partly or totally unlike in nature, form, or quality; not the same."

Different is a sacred word to me. I would even go as far to say Holy. The opposite of *normal*. *Different* is something to be desired. It is how you were designed, and thus, it is how you need to live.

When you see anything of excellence, the only way to describe it is *different*. You are attracted to different. Different inspires you. Different pulls you in. Consider the following:

- Championship teams are built differently. Think the 1990s Chicago Bulls, the 2000s New England Patriots, the 1980s U.S. Olympic hockey team.
- The best athletes in the world go about their business differently. Think Kobe Bryant, Michael Jordan, Serena Williams, Simone Biles, Tom Brady, and Deion Sanders.
- The most successful entrepreneurs operate differently. Think Oprah, Elon Musk, Walt Disney, Steve Jobs, Jeff Bezos, Beyonce, and Sara Blakely.
- Even the best marketing books say "don't be better, be different."

Entrepreneur Jesse Itzler tells a story about during his time building Marquis Jet when he was around many wealthy people. Some were healthy and many were not. He would ask the wealthy and healthy people how they lived so richly? That question had nothing to do with money, but everything to do with the abundance he saw in their life, and their answers were different than anything he had been exposed to before. They all responded, "It is because of my habits and health mentally, physically, spiritually, and emotionally." So he started asking:

- What time do you get up?
- What do you eat?
- How do you calm your mind?
- When do you go to sleep?
- What does a vacation look like?
- How do you exercise?
- How do you prioritize yourself?

As he gathered all this information on winning habits from people who looked different, thought differently, and had different results than most people, he began to implement them into his life. What worked, stuck. What didn't, he got rid of, and over time, he built this system of how he lived that worked for him. He intentionally built a life by design, something that allowed him to operate with a different level of focus, clarity, and energy to win.[19] It was inevitable because he chose a consistent life by design.

Now, imagine you could condense that time frame, and take out the guesswork of finding out the habits that actually worked for you and the ones that were possibly even holding you back or hurting you. That's why you are here.

You don't have to build a private jet company or invest countless years trying to get in front of these types of people like Jesse did, or be a professional athlete and have someone like me around to build your system for you. It lives right here in this book. I've built the system to create a personalized life by design right here. So you can live life differently and break free from the life of normal that is chasing after you and the relentless pursuit of everyone else.

You may think living differently is not accessible to you and that you have to accept the reality that you exist in every day. I am here to tell you that you don't. The most successful people in the world do not do anything extraordinary; what they did was the ordinary things with extraordinary consistency and intentionality. Which is different. Different was made exactly for you, but it requires you to take ownership. It requires you to realize that by choosing a life by design consistently, it is inevitable that you will experience different outcomes. There are only four mindsets that you can live with:

- Impossible
- Possible
- Probable
- Inevitable

I am here to tell you there is only one choice. Inevitable. The outcome is already predetermined. You will have the patience that is required to forgo what you want now for what you want most. Which again, takes you from normal to different. With a mindset of inevitability, if you were to improve your health by 1% every day for 365 days by the end of the year you are going to be 38% healthier. Small and consistent efforts are what powers inevitability, no matter how hard your journey seems. As you make the small changes consistently, you will make the big changes seem small. It's inevitable because you have chosen ownership. Commitment over convenience. Design over default. Different over normal.

Table 1.1

Normal	Different
Reactive	Proactive
Common	Uncommon
Average	Excellence
What the world says	What your body says
Life by default	Life by design
Earned illness	Earned health

There is a dichotomy between normal and different that is only accessible through ownership, but you must realize that normal will always pursue you. Check out Table 1.1.

As you choose to live differently, your reality begins to mirror everything that different includes. It does not discriminate and it does not play favorites. It is simply available for anyone who leans in.

My Path to Different

When I first arrived in the NHL to help manage the health and performance of the players, every player ate the same, trained the same, supplemented the same, recovered the same, and followed the same travel framework. Yet coaches and front office executives wondered why player illness and injury trends within the season were following the normal league trends. Just like you are wondering why your health is following the same trends that I mentioned earlier. Albert Einstein once said, "The definition of *insanity* is doing the same thing over and over, but expecting *different* results." The system was broken.

When I ask people to define *performance* for me, I get words like *success, winning, greatness,* and *execution.* The thing about that, however, is people are simply defining an outcome. An outcome that we don't always have control over. I define *performance* as the capacity and desire to intentionally and consistently behave at a level equal to your mental, physical, spiritual, and emotional potential. Everybody has the desire to perform, but what separates you from what you want to be is your capacity. Your capacity has to do with the system you have built. How intentional and consistent is it? It is likely you have not designed it, but rather fallen into it by default, which is why your system has been built for failure. It's inevitable you are going to get an outcome; you can't control that. What you can control, however, is the process on the way there, and then the outcome you desire becomes inevitable over time because your outcomes are the lagging effect of your consistent habits and behaviors. But there is an important thing you need to understand: health precedes performance.

It was not until the team I was working with allowed me to approach things differently and build different systems that we began to see different results. We started measuring things like heart rate variability (HRV), blood biochemistry, and key performance metrics during training so we could learn more about what was truly going on in each player's body. The cellular deficiencies, high levels of internal stress loads, and daily biometric data variations provided unique opportunities for player, coach, and management education, while allowing us to explore what specific habits were applicable for each player individually. For the first time in their careers, our players were given individualized sleep routines, individualized supplement routines, individualized nutrition guidelines, and training programs that were adapted to their specific level of readiness. We were treating players differently based on what they needed, not out of convenience or because "that is how it was normally done."

Unsurprisingly, we soon witnessed a different level of buy-in, as players saw their personal data being used to tailor habits and all aspects of their life on and off the ice. They felt empowered. And guess what? Our illness and injury rates dropped significantly. The outcome was inevitable, and simply a reflection of our system. Suddenly, everyone wanted to know what we were doing differently.

The mistake I made was that I was doing it for everyone around me, but I was not doing it for myself, and it almost cost me my life. Today, I continue to work with top athletes across the pro leagues. They are seeking to be different in every corner of their lives.

It is well publicized that LeBron James spends $1.5 million a year to proactively prepare his mind and body differently, but it's the small consistent daily choices that nobody sees, like packing snacks to eat at his sons' games instead of eating what is around him, that truly set him apart. He doesn't get IVs and then fail to drink enough water. He doesn't get in the hyperbaric or red-light bed and then sleep five hours a night. That's what a normal person does, but he is different.

Patrick Mahomes has a consistent sleep time of 9:30–10:00 p.m. each night, paired with a consistent 7 a.m. wake-up call to optimize his circadian rhythm. He eats five meals each day, adhering to specific serving sizes and sequencing to optimize his blood sugar and recovery.

Mookie Betts, arguably the most consistent MLB player over the past five years, packs a separate suitcase for road trips with utensils, cooking supplies, and food so that he can make sure his intake is not disrupted by travel.

What do these three athletes have in common?

They are willing to take ownership of their bodies and recognize the power of doing things differently.

They have a mindset of inevitability and know all they need to do is be consistent because they have their personalized plan in a life by design.

They have awareness to see the dysfunction most of the others around them make excuses about and call normal.

They are willing to stand out and be different.

They lean on data, not opinion, to steer the habits they intentionally make a priority.

They invest in elite expertise to manage their personal health and performance success to provide accountability and community.

You may not be a pro athlete. But just like them you need your health in order to perform. You can make the choice to be different. You can choose a personalized solution and a life by design over what the world tells you and a life by default. You can focus not on the outcome, but on the process of consistency. You can adopt the mindset of inevitability and know deep down that you are already on your way to true health. You also now have the same systems and processes available to the best athletes in the world available to you. Your health precedes your performance, so it's time to start living differently.

Health: A Human Problem, Not an Athlete Problem

During what turned out to be my last year in the NHL, I fielded a call from an owner of another NHL team (let's call him Frank). Frank had heard about some of the things we were doing differently with our players and he asked if we could meet for lunch while they were in town for a game against us. I said "yes" and immediately started reading everything I could find about him. I looked at pictures and read about his entrepreneurial journey and the impact he had made. What he had accomplished so much in his 61 years was incredibly impressive. I couldn't imagine why he wanted to meet with me, other than to see what I might be willing to share about our program.

I arrived first to the Orange County restaurant where we had agreed to meet for lunch. Suddenly I heard my name called to the left of me: "Justin, great to see you." I had to do a double-take because this was not the same guy I had read about online. This man looked at least 20 years older. I stood up and greeted him and we immediately got down to business. He opened, "I wanted to meet because I have been hearing about what you are doing around player health management, and honestly, I feel like I have aged 20 years in the past 12 months. I'm exhausted and do not feel well, yet my doctors tell me I am the picture of health for my age. Can you help me?"

After that meeting, Frank and I began working together. Six months later his cholesterol had dropped 50% into a healthy range and he was able to go off his medication; his pre-diabetic blood sugar levels had dropped below 5.5 for the first time in a decade, and his heart rate variability (we will learn more about this in Chapter 4) went from a daily average of 21 to 68. More importantly, he was aware of the dysfunctional behaviors he had normalized for years simply because it was what everyone else around him was doing. With that, he was able to design a life that was different.

A life that limited the unnecessary stress on his body, redeemed his health, and left normal behind.

It was at that moment that I realized what I was doing for my hockey players was something everyone needed: a life by design. Health is not just an athlete thing. It's a human thing. Either you prioritize your health or you will be forced to prioritize your illness. The National Institute on Aging and Disease conducted several studies that looked at the impact of behavior change on longevity. It showed that the majority of chronic illnesses could be prevented by establishing consistent long-term positive habits and behavior change. The complete opposite of what the world tells us.

I experienced that realization and so did Frank. It became my mission to solve the stress and health issues plaguing entrepreneurs, business leaders, and executive teams so that they can lead differently and realize their missions while impacting millions of people. I wanted to make available the systems that are typically only available to elite athletes. Things like testing, technology, education, and coaching, so you too can optimize your health and live life by design.

Do not confuse optimization with perfection. Do not confuse consistency with perfection. Optimization is the pursuit of better. Optimized health and a life by design are not a destination, but a journey, and by just pursuing it, you will inevitably result in improvement.

Why would you accept less than and settle for what is normal? You do everything you can to optimize your business, knowing that your business will never be perfect, and by pursuing it you have seen the inevitable results, but you don't do that for the one thing that impacts the quality of your reality, and you are in control of the choice.

No longer should it be acceptable for you to live comfortably in dysfunction, seeking quick fixes and calling it normal, while at the same time, expecting to be at your best and get elite level results. Without health, you will never realize the energy level, focus, stamina, or results you desire, and even worse, losing health costs you your life.

Since helping myself and Frank, hundreds of Fortune 500 companies, business leaders, and entrepreneurs have leaned on us. Without fail, we awaken people with their own data, and introduce them to new strategies for self-healing and self-empowerment so they can embrace *different*. The sad reality about normal is that you don't know what different feels like because normal is all you know. It's not until you are willing to try something different that you realize how dead normal is. It's only then do you take ownership of your life, build a life by design, and embrace *different*, realizing being normal becomes something you want as much distance from as possible.

Living differently creates *different* results. Whether those results are in business, family, or health. When you see something *different*, it changes your perspective. It opens up new possibilities. It gives you permission to raise your bar. It is my hope that this book will be your wake-up call. To help you realize:

- Yes, it is possible to have a successful business and your health.
- Yes, it is possible to be a great mom or dad and have your health.
- Yes, it is possible to be an impactful leader and have your health.

- Yes, it is possible to have rich relationships and your health.
- Yes, it is possible to travel, be immersed in all that the world has to offer, and still have your health.

But it requires looking at things differently. And it starts with how you look at stress.

2

A Different Approach to Stress

*"If you want things to be different, perhaps the answer is to
become different yourself."*
—Norman Vincent Peale

How DO THE same problems impact a fit 28-year-old and an
experienced 61-year-old (as I describe in Chapter 1)? The
same way they will impact you if a life by design is not created. The monster that caught me is after you, and leaves
behind a path of burnout, chronic illness, sickness, and
health destruction. The monster's name is Stress, and I'm
going to show you how you approach it differently. In the
United States, we hope for health, but we incentivize for
illness. All of the money lies in waiting for you and your
dysfunctional habits, which society has told you are normal,
to lead you right into illness and then making money to try

and heal you. It led me to ask the question, "What would different look like?"

Understanding the Body's Responses to Stress

I was sitting in my doctorate-level cellular biology class when everything came together for me. We had just begun talking about cellular healing and were working through some definitions to establish clarity. The definition for *heal* was the exact same as the definition for *integrated*: "to bring everything together or to make one." When you combine that with that concept that *holistic* means "all or everything" and that our health comprises the mental, physical, spiritual, and emotional condition, it becomes pretty clear that, in order to establish health, you needed to look at everything as one, which is also how stress works in our bodies.

I am not talking about the frazzled pull-your-hair-out stress you feel when you are running after your Uber driver who is leaving without you as you're late for the airport. Instead, I am talking about the simple daily stressors you take for granted that your body is constantly paying the price to adapt to. Things like filtering the air you breathe; digesting the food you eat; and managing your physical, mental, emotional, and spiritual fluctuations of the day.

Your body has a few stress mechanisms that are critical to understand:

- It doesn't know the difference among mental, physical, spiritual, and emotional stress, which is why you need to treat them as one.
- It cannot dissociate between real or perceived stress.

- It doesn't know the difference between positive and negative stress.[1]

Your body was designed to keep you alive, and thus, produce a stress response to any form of real or perceived; positive or negative; mental, physical, spiritual, or emotional stress.

Because of those mechanisms, you can begin to understand how easy it is to be in a constant state of chronic stress. Especially as a business owner, parent, spouse, or any other position of leadership, where many of these forms seem to be completely out of our control. The autonomic nervous system is what makes those mechanisms function and has two primary responses that you need to know about.

- One is called the sympathetic nervous system (fight, flight, freeze). It is activated during any real, perceived, positive, negative, mental, physical, spiritual, or emotional stressor. Our brains were built and wired to keep us alive, which is why the sympathetic nervous system is so sensitive and often hyperactive. It causes an increase in heart rate; increase in respiration rate; dilation of the pupils; increase in hormones like epinephrine, norepinephrine, cortisol, and adrenaline; while decreasing non-lifesaving actions like digestion.
- The other is called the parasympathetic nervous system (rest, digest, relax). It is activated when there is no perceived threat or stressor the body is aware of. It is possible to bring yourself to this state through self-regulation and awareness.[2]

The interaction between these two systems is like a water faucet, and our body is the cup. There are varying speeds at which stress flows, not simply on or off. There are seasons in each of our lives when the water coming from the faucet is dripping and there are seasons when it is flowing quickly, which is why finding balance in life just doesn't exist; you have to find a *rhythm*. Either way, each of our cups have a certain capacity before they overflow. This analogy highlights there are only two ways you can prevent the cup from overflowing.

- Turn down the faucet.
- Poke holes in our cup to allow it to drain.

In your life, it's often out of your control as to whether you can turn down the water flow, but you 100% have control of how many holes are in your cup. These are your habits, behaviors, and lifestyle choices. Purposeful habits and behaviors facilitate the activation of the parasympathetic nervous system and bring you into a recovery state, which allows the cup to drain and take on more stress sustainably. We call that resiliency! *Resiliency* is "the ability to develop a capacity to withstand or recover quickly from stress or difficulties." Figure 2.1 illustrates this concept in more detail.

By understanding that our body is constantly under stress and that there is no dissociation among mental, emotional, spiritual, and physical stressors, it is easy to see how overwhelmed our system can be just because of our normal routines. This is where we begin to help you take a different approach, disrupt the dysfunctional patterns, and establish life by design.

Life by Default   Life by Design

Figure 2.1 Filling and draining your cup.

Source: OWN IT Coaching / Justin Roethlingshoefer.

Introducing the Four Quadrants to Find Your Rhythm

The rhythm that you want to establish shows up in the Life by Design Quadrants in Figure 2.2 and provides a powerful visual for what health looks and feels like so you can leverage the power of ownership.

Here are the four quadrants shown in Figure 2.2:

- *Overreaching Quadrant:* In this quadrant, you are exposed to various intensities of intermediate or temporary stress, be it mental, emotional, spiritual, or physical, and activates the sympathetic nervous system. In scientific terms that is the definition for *hormesis.* This is the quadrant that represents most of everyday life stress like running a business or raising a

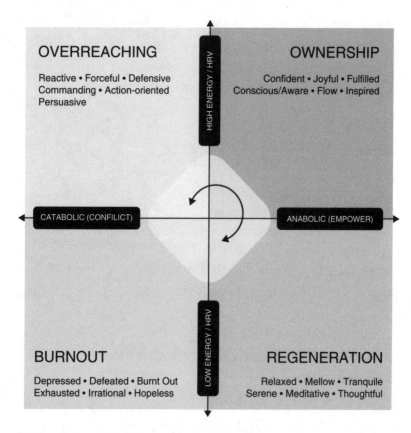

OVERREACHING

Reactive • Forceful • Defensive
Commanding • Action-oriented
Persuasive

OWNERSHIP

Confident • Joyful • Fulfilled
Conscious/Aware • Flow • Inspired

HIGH ENERGY / HRV

CATABOLIC (CONFILICT)

ANABOLIC (EMPOWER)

LOW ENERGY / HRV

BURNOUT

Depressed • Defeated • Burnt Out
Exhausted • Irrational • Hopeless

REGENERATION

Relaxed • Mellow • Tranquile
Serene • Meditative • Thoughtful

Figure 2.2   The Life by Design Quadrants.

Source: OWN IT Coaching / Justin Roethlingshoefer.

family, along with the stressors that you seek like workouts, intermittent fasting, sauna, and cold tubs. Some of these stressors you can add strategically or in a periodized way depending on the season of life so that the faucet is not always fully open. Think about this as adjusting the speed of water coming into your cup.

- **Regeneration Quadrant:** In this quadrant, you are exposed to various techniques that increase the activation of the parasympathetic nervous system (rest/digest/relax). This quadrant puts you in a relaxed, tranquil, and recovery-based state. In scientific terms, this process is called *allostasis*, which is the adaptation to meet perceived and anticipated demands from stress. You need to intentionally invest time here in order to recover and grow your capacity. Think about this as the amount and size of the holes in your cup.
- **Ownership Quadrant:** This is the quadrant where you want to experience life. I call this the "when life is working" quadrant. You operate in this quadrant when you find the appropriate rhythm between overreaching and regeneration. You don't stay in this quadrant all the time, but rather feel energized, alert, focused, and confident when you operate here.
- **Burnout/Blow up Quadrant:** This quadrant, unfortunately, is where the vast majority of you live. The longer you operate in the overreaching quadrant, the more often you experience this quadrant due to the chronic stress overload. When you live here for too long, it eventually causes chronic health issues.

Out of Rhythm: Too Much Overreaching

It is so common to experience stressors in every health domain—mental, emotional, spiritual, and physical—all at once. You are growing a business, raising a family, getting married, trying to get fit, and experiencing high levels of stress that are never ceasing. You tell yourself it is just a season, but the season lasts for three years. That is not a season; it is a lifestyle. If you are honest, it's a lifestyle that is slowly killing you, leaving you sick, overwhelmed, and exhausted in the meantime. It's the dysfunctional rhythm that many of you consider normal. Your outcomes are simply a lagging result of your habits, behaviors, and lifestyle.

In the Chapter 1 examples, we saw me and Frank begin to identify the health issues that were created by living a life that was prioritized by chronic overreaching. In me, it was the constant time zone changes, low sleep quality, continual pull of wanting to be with my family or business when I was with the team, or with the team when I was with my family or business, and working long hours without any regard for how I was doing. Even my workouts, although a healthy habit to establish, were a stressor that my body then had to adapt to. The constant barrage and flow of stress caused my cup to overflow for so long that my body had no choice but to break. My break was ulcers and polyps that caused fatigue, bloating, and stomach pain.

Frank's issues came from the years of mental and emotional stress of building four businesses and having over 3,000 employees around the country. His shortage of sleep, poor diet, alcohol intake, lack of physical fitness, and time for himself caused the heavy overflow and led to his break. The unique part, however, is doctors masked his break for a long time with medication, and when you do that, it is like putting a Band-Aid® on a bullet hole thinking it is healed, only eventually causing you to bleed out. Your break may be something totally different, but it stems from the same monster: stress.

Out of Rhythm: Too Much Regeneration

Too much regeneration is a little less common, but has equal cause in burnout and development of chronic health issues because of the inability to handle stressors. The decay in your health and acceleration of aging comes from what I call the *aggressive pursuit of comfort*, which can only be prevented by being exposed to stress and the overreaching quadrant. The more established you get and the more successful you become, the more your pursuit of comfort will increase, unless you design it differently.

It has been shown that by avoiding stress, your life expectancy dramatically drops due to the increase in stress for very simple tasks.[3] The less developed you are in an area, the more susceptible to burnout, illness, and disease you are, so you have to find your rhythm. It's why you'll see some people who worked all their life, were active, and then retired, became sedentary, and didn't participate in hobbies that elicit stress have their health and well-being dramatically deteriorate at an exponential rate. When you stop exercising at intensities that are uncomfortable, when you eat at the slightest twinge of hunger, when you sit in air conditioned or heated homes and never experience dramatic temperature fluctuations, your body stops having to adapt, you become less resilient, and easier to kill. Stress can be a weapon if you know how to design a rhythm.

When you can establish a rhythm intentionally, you will notice an increase in capacity and ability to handle stress, but when you don't, it causes chronic stress overload that you will notice the opposite effect. We call this the stress adaptation cycle. In Figure 2.3, you can see how important

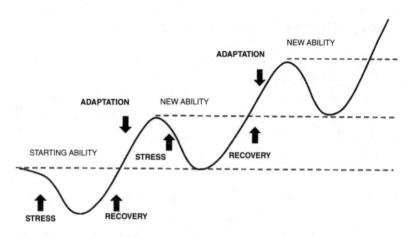

Figure 2.3   Regeneration and recovery.
© *John Wiley & Sons, Inc.*

the regeneration and recovery time is to health growth and capacity. Yet, we continue to ignore it.

Recognizing That It"s Hard to Find a Rhythm

Why is it so hard to establish a sustainable rhythm? You know the results you want, but they have always seemingly been out of reach. It's because you have only ever tried what was normal in your family, industry, or environment. When you operate from that narrative, your rhythm will never be your own and results will never be different.

One of my first corporate clients was a hedge fund in New York City. The CEO of the hedge fund—let's call him Barry—had come to me asking if I could help his day traders. Over the last three years, he had seen a turnover in day traders that was unacceptable for his industry and a burnout rate that was concerning to him. It was impacting their energy, mental clarity, and focus, which also was having the same impact on him.

As we met the team and put frameworks in place to help optimize those areas, we heard the same things repeatedly. "It's normal in our industry to eat late, be out four nights a week with clients, have a few drinks daily, and get five hours of sleep. How do we implement the changes you are asking for and break what's normal?"

Simple. Choose *different* over *normal*.

Barry was fully supportive of the changes we proposed and embraced something that was completely different for the industry and the culture he had established over the last 25 years in business. He redesigned his office space and put in a smoothie bar, gym, saunas, float tanks, cold plunges, red-light and meditation rooms, but in a way where meetings could be the focal point. The normal dinner meetings and late evening networking events turned into workout meetings, or wellness networking events with smoothies, saunas, cold plunges, and steam rooms at the company's facility in downtown Manhattan. The company provided bonuses and days off driven by sleep quality and heart rate variability metrics (see Chapter 4).

As we started implementing these changes, clients took notice. Not only did the health and energy levels of their traders change, but the bottom line started to change as well. The company's clients preferred this *different* way of doing business and valued a *different* approach. People preferred doing business with the company because the traders were more alert and more focused. But also, the same problem that Barry was trying to solve was plaguing his clients as well. By simply being around Barry and his team, his clients began to see a change in their health. That is what choosing to do things differently can do. It makes people take notice, allows you to stand out, and that is something that you want when it is for the right reasons.

All Barry did was make an adjustment in how he empowered his day traders to do business. He changed the environment and put some frameworks in place so that his trading team could invest more time regenerating, and he took it upon himself to make it available. As you can imagine the issue of burnout and turnover quickly went away, and the rhythm of the entire office was reestablished.

Establishing Your Different

Today, more than ever before, people just like you are demanding something different when it comes to their health, but the road to get there is full of confusion. This is where another side of normal is found: the health, wellness, and biohacking industry. The hyperactive culture where you are inundated with the latest and greatest tools, technology, testing, or supplements that will transform your health. However, many of you reading this may be saying, "Justin, I have tried every biohack and health product available but nothing has helped." It is no wonder why the $4.7-trillion health and wellness industry is growing exponentially, but is still missing the opportunity to prevent burnout, sickness, illness, and disease. Anyone with their health has hundreds of goals, but someone without their health simply has one. That's why we need to empower you, and it starts with helping you understand stress.

First off, you are not broken; you are just out of rhythm.

Second, you are not alone. You have fallen victim to the health and wellness industry, and unfortunately, even in an industry that is supposed to be helping you, you need to be different. What the world tells you is healthy may be hurting you, while what works for others may actually be killing you. Even though the modality, tool, or supplement may work, it may still not be right for you.

Sifting through the Data

I was standing with a group of attendees after one of my keynotes in Atlanta three months ago and one of them asked, "How do you have the energy and look how you do with how much you travel and work? I have tried everything you do, but can't get the results, what am I doing wrong?"

So I asked him, "What do you think it is that I am doing, and what have you tried?"

He began to get a little red in the face and went on to explain that he had heard on a podcast the benefits of cold plunging so he bought one, while forcing himself to get in everyday because it was healthy. He was at a conference and a well-known biohacking speaker talked about a DNA and blood test, so he got that done and had 12 different supplements coming to his house every month. His co-worker had dropped 30 pounds at a local CrossFit gym, so he joined as well. One of his favorite fitness influencers had done some posts on a wearable device, so he bought one of those and began looking at the data. His wife had read a book on intermittent fasting and he abided by that routine. By the time he finished explaining everything he tried to do for his body, he said he was spending close to $2,000/month on his health that he was seeing no return on, and was even more confused and frustrated.

When I asked him what he understood about his body or what he had learned, his answer summed up everything for me. "Nothing, I am more confused than ever. I am getting sick more now than I was before and have no energy."

It's the same position that you likely find yourself in, or eventually will.

Nothing that he was doing was innately wrong. All of the interventions, testing, and technology he was trying are great, but the problem is that he was not looking at how his interventions were impacting his rhythm of stress. Was it improving his overreaching and regeneration cycle or making it worse? In this case, making it worse. Trying to implement what was normal in the industry but causing dysfunction for him.

I want to reiterate, he was not doing anything wrong; however, he was engaging in some things that were wrong for him at the time. He was taking actions that he didn't understand how they would impact his body, and because he did not understand the information coming back, he didn't know how to adapt and make the change.

So I felt convicted that I was supposed to talk with this person and help him.

The first thing I asked was to see his wearable data. When I looked at his heart rate variability (or HRV; more on that in Chapter 4), his week average was 21, his month average was 23, and his three-month average was 27. This is an extremely successful and what many would call fit, 39-year-old male business owner. The data indicated a long-term downward trend, meaning that his sympathetic nervous system or fight/flight/stress system is more active than his parasympathetic nervous system or rest/digest/relax system. His rhythm was off, and thus causing his body's cup to continue to get filled up and be in a chronic state of stress.

When I explained HRV to him, his eyes all of a sudden lit up, "You mean a higher number is better, and I overall want to see a trend upward over time? I have just been looking at the different colors and scores not knowing what they meant." That was exactly it. You see the tech companies have had to create fancy algorithms, scores, and graphs to generate an intellectual property (IP) that made them worth something, while in the process, only confused the consumer more. In doing so, they got further away from the raw number that gave quality information and made understanding it simple and actionable.

When we dove into HRV further, we were able to pinpoint days that had low HRV scores, and again his eyes got big because when he corresponded his calendar with the data, he saw things like, a travel day, a day that he got almost no sleep because his daughter was sick, a day that he uncovered a partner was laundering money in his business, and a day that he ran a marathon. These were all elevated forms of stress—mental, physical, spiritual, and emotional—that all showed up in the data, that he never adjusted habits or behaviors to make up for what was asked of his body because he was unaware, and simply did not know . . . even though the information was in front of him all the time.

Next, we went to his sleep data. We saw that he was sleeping about seven hours a night, but constantly woke up tired. His quality sleep (slow wave and REM sleep) made up about 35% of his average sleep time. The goal should be around 50%. When we discussed this, for the third time his eyes widened because he thought getting seven hours of sleep was all that mattered. So we talked about what his sleep habits looked like. He would typically eat a snack right before bed, it wasn't uncommon for him to be sending emails at 10 p.m. to his clients and team on the West Coast, he and his wife would fall asleep with the TV on, and his wife liked it hotter in the room than he preferred. Immediately, we figured out some key behavior changes that would have saved him about $8,000 on that new mattress that promised him the best night sleep ever. We talked about stopping eating three hours before bed, putting a boundary on when he would stop working, put a snooze timer on the TV, and got a thermoregulator for his bed so that he could sleep cool and his wife could sleep warm.

When we went back to his HRV numbers and began to correlate his lowest days to his poorest sleeping days, there was a high correlated value. Thus, he was able to understand that his body was in a chronic stress state because of his constant poor sleep quality due to his habits. Immediately, there was a new motivation to create change and try something different.

When I began to talk about stress, he brought up the cold tub. The thing about the cold tub is that it is another stressor on the body, I explained. The benefits are great, but for someone who is prepared for it. It is like going for an expensive dinner. The food is great, and the ambience is awesome, but if you don't have the money to pay for the bill, it takes something that was positive and turns it negative. Same with the cold tub. He was under chronic stress, and thus, adding another stressor was only adding more water to his cup that had no capacity left. Also, he had the temperature at 34°F, which for a beginner was far too cold and far too stressful. We put a protocol in place where he turned the temperature up to 50°F, and went in only on days that his HRV was above his week average. Every week, he could turn it down a degree if he desired.

When we looked at his DNA and blood testing, I asked him, "What changed in your diet and lifestyle when you saw these?" Again he said, "Nothing, I just have 32 pages of pdfs and follow intermittent fasting since my wife said it was healthy." When we talked about intermittent fasting, he said he was fasting until 3 p.m. and eating until bedtime. We discussed the added stress to his body early in the day and then how the late-night eating was impacting his sleep quality and circadian rhythm. By shifting his time-restricted eating window to three hours after waking and three hours before he goes to bed, not only would it enable him to have more energy throughout the day, but it would decrease stress levels and help him with sleep quality at night. The other thing we identified was that he would eat really well at home, but when he traveled, he would go off the rails because he didn't know what to focus on. His testing came back showing a need for more protein in his diet, and some of his micronutrient deficiencies required a greater variety of vegetables at meals. Empowered, he now knew what to look at and what to avoid when on the road.

Last, when we talked about his gym routine, he would go to CrossFit and kill himself and then take three days off because he was so sore, which again would skyrocket his stress levels. I encouraged him to increase the number of times to three days a week and invest three other days a week doing 25 minutes of zone 2 conditioning at a heart rate of 120–135 beats per minute. It would increase his aerobic fitness while also helping with some of the soreness he was experiencing. Long-term consistency over short-term intensity.

After about 30 minutes, the frustrated look he showed up with was completely gone, and his demeanor was one of hope, clarity, and understanding. He said, "Thank you so much; for the first time, I feel like I understand what I am looking at and know what to do and to look for."

Realizing That Different Works

What the world tells you is healthy may actually be holding you back. It is not just about more information. In fact, in many cases, it could be about less information. You need to better understand what you are looking at, while being educated, guided, and taught how to apply it. Ownership is the intersection point of taking responsibility and accountability. You need to push for something different even within the health industry. The medical system and doctors don't have time for that, the registered dietitians and functional medicine practitioners don't have the resources to do it, and the tech companies can't build the relationships because trust and relationships are human to human. This is why this book exists. To educate, empower, and help you do things differently.

A month later, I reached out to the man I had met at the end of the conference. I was really interested to see how he was doing and what his results were. Within 30 seconds of hitting send, I got a response that had two words: LIFE CHANGING. He proceeded to tell me he had lost 11 pounds, his stress levels that he didn't even know were elevated felt manageable, he hadn't been sick all month even when a flu ripped through his office, he was sleeping better than ever, and his quality was up to 54% even with a drop in total sleep duration because of a busy season in his life. For the first time, he felt like he had control over his body and how he felt. Two years later, he is still a client, and we have only been able to go deeper and more specific to him with strategies.

It is not about more information. It's about being able to apply the information in a personalized way that means something for you. To be able to manage the stress that your body is having to adapt to holistically so your body can be in rhythm. The way to do that is by educating and empowering you so you can make different decisions with confidence and live a life by design.

3

Your Body Has a Language

"Symptoms are the body's mother tongue; signs are in a different language."

—John Brown

As MY WIFE and I were getting ready to take off for our honeymoon to Vietnam, we called over the flight attendant to ask where we would go after we landed, as it would be our first time. She encouraged us as we got off the plane in Vietnam to get through customs as fast as possible to get our shuttle to the resort. We looked at each other and agreed that it should be fairly simple as she delegated me to carry the bags and she would direct us.

After a smooth 19-hour flight, we landed in Vietnam. A gorgeous country, and if you have not been, it is definitely worth the trip. As I gathered up our bags from the overhead compartment and Alyse grabbed our passports, we walked off the plane. It was as soon as we stepped off the plane that we began to run into issues. The signs were in Vietnamese, the staff and military we asked for directions only spoke Vietnamese, and there were no diagrams or pictures that we could understand to help us get to customs as quickly as possible like we were instructed.

Immediately, I began to feel panicked, anxious, overwhelmed, and frustrated. Then, in that exact same moment, I realized that is how our bodies feel about us. You don't speak the language of your body. You have not been trained to. No matter how many different ways your body tries to communicate, it begins to feel frustrated, overwhelmed, anxious, and panicked.

As human beings, we have multiple forms of language we use every single day to communicate. We have body language, spoken language, and physical touch language. Our bodies also have those multiple forms of language, like symptoms and reactions, but we often ignore them, think they are normal, or become gaslit into believing that we are not actually experiencing what we are feeling, and go right back to the life of default we were living in.

Unfortunately, often you don't become aware until you have a wake-up call. What do I mean by this? You may be sitting there reading this, saying, "No, Justin, I feel relatively healthy. I wake up and work out every day. I don't feel overly tired throughout the day. I sleep well. I feel pretty good for 45." Conceptually, you may be right. But you have no idea what your body is saying. You have no idea what your body is trying to communicate to you because you have a distorted view of normal. You don't know what different feels like. For 45 years (or however old you are), your body has been writing checks to pay the price for all the stressors you have been exposing it to. You have been living by default in a rhythm that is not right for you. I've seen too often the wake-up call comes in the form of a heart attack, stroke, panic attack, mental breakdown, diagnosis of diabetes, heart disease, or cancer because you did not have the awareness leading up. Or even worse, you did have awareness and chose not to prioritize it, ignored it, and exacerbated the issue.

I don't want that to be your wake-up call. I want your wake-up call to be today. I want this chapter to call out your life by default and help you walk into a life by design built for you, but it will require you to be honest so you can recognize how your body is trying to communicate with you, and be empowered to make a change and get out of your life of default. I want you to be your own advocate, take ownership of your health, find your own rhythm, and live a life by design.

There are three ways that your body is communicating with you every single day and different ways to make you aware of it. Awareness makes problems lose their power over you. The things that you felt were out of your control—the energy loss, the fatigue, the anxiety, the weight gain—suddenly seem surmountable because you have a newfound awareness as to where they originated. You have a newfound hope in controlling what matters to you because you have a way to guide your habits and behaviors. As you go through the following three signs of a life in default, honesty is the best way to identify where you are, generate awareness, and experience the wake-up call you need. Otherwise, you'll simply keep your head in the sand, continue to live by default, and wait for your illness or disease to wake you up. So let's get honest.

Sign 1 of a Life in Default: Stress Adds Up

As I landed in Dallas for a workshop I was leading, I stopped at the Dallas-Fort Worth airport rental car area. It was an extremely busy weekend and the only rentals they had available were Teslas and Kias. So I chose the Tesla and proceeded to make my way to north Texas. As a non-Tesla owner, I did not exactly understand every aspect of the vehicle. I had rented a few before, but my wife had always been there with me, and I am not ashamed to say she is the tech guru of the family.

With a fully charged battery, I was not thinking about anything other than getting to my destination. I adjusted the mirrors, cranked the air conditioning, plugged in the directions, and connected my phone to the Bluetooth for music just as I would any other vehicle. As I put my foot on the pedal and took off, I suddenly remembered how much I loved the smooth ride. It would accelerate so quickly, and even at 90+ mph, it felt like you were gliding, and on the rural roads of North Texas where there was not a soul to be seen, it was extremely freeing.

As I arrived at the Wildcatter Ranch, I had 39% left on the charge. I got out of the car and asked the ranger if they had a supercharger on the ranch and if I could use it. The look on their faces said it all as they responded with a laugh, "Not a chance." So I plugged it in using the cable and a normal outlet, thinking the 36 hours I was there would be more than enough time to get it back to a charge that would take me back to the airport.

As I got into the car 36 hours later, the battery read 43%. Shocked but also extremely confused at the same time, I got in and proceeded to do the same thing I did when I got in the car at the airport. As I typed in the address to get to the airport, the car's GPS naturally directed me to the nearest supercharger. Feeling much more confident that I was going to have enough charge, I sat down and began driving. About five miles into the trip, I noticed the GPS rerouted me, and then three minutes later, rerouted me again. Panicked, I began to drive faster, thinking I needed to get to the destination before the charge ran out. As I sped up I saw the percentage tick downward 19%. . .18%. . .17%. I got rerouted one more time. This time a big red bar came across the top of the map that said there was not enough power to make it to the next supercharger; find a charging outlet asap.

I was in the middle of nowhere Texas surrounded by nothing but gas and oil sources, with a vehicle that did not use anything to run except electricity. As I tried to make it to the closest town, my route took me to Jacksboro, Texas, a town of 4,100 people, and stopped at a Ford dealership that also doubled as a grocery store and barber shop. I stopped with 2% charge left on the car, and needed 4% to get me to the next supercharger. I pulled out the trusty charging cord and plugged it into the wall outlet just like I had done back at Wildcatter Ranch. My flight was scheduled to leave in three hours and I had virtual keynotes and webinars back to back that I had originally planned to do in the airport lounge. Not anymore. Plans had changed.

Everything officially had come to a halt. Four hours later I got to 4% charge. I got back in the car, and a warning sign appeared on the screen. I had become hypersensitive to the alerts because of the experience of the past six hours, and it said "keep under 50 mph to make it to the next supercharging station." Well, wouldn't that have been helpful six hours ago when I was leaving Wildcatter! As I got to the supercharger,

I had 1% charge left. I attached it to the appropriate power source and within 35 minutes it was back to 100%, but I had missed my flight, completed my keynote and the webinar in the bathroom at the dealership, and had to take a red-eye flight back home to Miami. What was a terrible situation turned out to be a story that generated an extremely powerful analogy for our health.

Your Body Needs to Recharge

Your body is exactly like that Tesla, and you don't understand it. My first mistake was trying to get to a destination in a car I didn't understand, but yet you do that every single day with your body. You don't know what is working well or what is not. If I had understood the car well, I would have been aware that the air conditioning, screen brightness, Bluetooth, phone charging station, fast accelerations, and speeds above a certain level all drew battery from the charge, and it wasn't like a gas vehicle pulling energy from different sources. Again, just like your body. You don't have different sources to pull energy from. Mental, physical, spiritual, and emotional stress all pull from the same source, and our bodies have to pay the price to adapt to it.

When you are unaware of the stressors, they catch up to you. You fall ill, you gain weight, you suffer brain fog, you can't sleep, you have no energy, you don't feel well, and you blame it on the most recent thing that happened, when in fact, it was because you didn't have the right charging station. You didn't give yourself the time and space necessary to properly recover. You had stressors in your life pulling energy from you that kept you in the overreaching quadrant with no rhythm (see Chapter 2). Then life suddenly stops.

Life gets shut down. You don't prioritize your health and now you are forced to prioritize your illness.

You design your day so well around your business, but yet fail to design your day around the vehicles that run them, your body. I had designed my day beautifully. I was going to make all my calls, and make my flight, while getting everywhere I needed to go, but I had failed to plan around the vehicle that was taking me there. And suddenly, it was too late.

Even as I got to a full charge on the car, I turned down the screen brightness, I rolled down the windows instead of using the AC, paranoid I would run out of battery again, not trusting the vehicle nor understanding the information it was giving me. I was not using the car the way it was designed or what it was built to do.

Again, just like your health. You are designed for stress, designed to take it on at intermittent intervals, but you don't understand how to prepare it to handle the stress, nor how to design your life with a rhythm between stress and recovery, like I explain in Chapter 2. You don't rise to the level of your goals; you fall to the level of your systems. Some of you have systems in place that lead to that failure, like the audience member at my keynote that I talk about in Chapter 2. You have systematic habits that will lead to external failures. Some systems are responsible for success, but others are simply limiting your capacity. The only way to mitigate those habits, be it mental, physical, spiritual, or emotional, is to have a way to measure them, understand them, and make a decision to change them. To live a life of design. To live differently.

If the Tesla had a bigger battery or held a charge longer and was more efficient, I would not have had an issue. Same with your body. If you have a greater capacity to take on stress and process it, you would have resilience that is far greater than what is exuded today. That doesn't mean just pushing through and doing more, but rather understanding what it needs and living in the stress to recover rhythm.

The Holmes and Rahe Stress Scale

Psychiatrists Thomas Holmes and Richard Rahe conducted a study in 1967 that looked at different life events and were able to create a predictable model as to whether or not there was a susceptibility to health breakdown in the next two years.[1] As Chapter 2 discusses, when it comes to stress, our bodies don't know the difference among mental, physical, spiritual, or emotional stress; cannot dissociate between positive or negative, real or perceived stressors; thus, leaving everything in our lives to contribute to either an increase in how fast our cup is filling up or how many holes are present, allowing them to drain.

What Holmes and Rahe did was create a weighting system based on the different life stressors you experienced over the past year and generate a total based on the listed stressors you had experienced. The interesting component of the list is that there are mental, physical, spiritual, and emotional stressors. There are positive and negative stressors. There are real and perceived stressors. What the study found was that if you had a total score of below 150, you had a low susceptibility of health breakdown, mental, physical, spiritual, or emotional in the next two years. If you scored between 150 and 300, you had a 50% chance of health breakdown in the next two years. And if you had a score over 300, you had a high susceptibility to health breakdown in the next two years.

The astonishing part is that when they validated the study across multiple populations, cultures, age ranges, and careers, they were able to accurately predict it within 3%. When we began using this in each of our workshops for businesses and leadership teams, not only did we also find high levels of correlation, but also incredibly high reliability when compared to heart rate variability scores (more information on HRV comes later in this book).

Just like in the earlier story with the Tesla, it is your responsibility to be aware of what is drawing from you and what is filling up your cup with stress. I want you to take the Holmes and Rahe assessment and generate awareness:

Instructions: Circle the totals of the life events you have experienced over the previous year. Total them at the bottom.

Death of spouse 100	Major business adjustment 39	Troubles with the boss 23
Divorce 75	Major change in financial state (better or worse) 39	Major change in work hours or conditions 20
Marital or relationship breakup or separation 65	Death of a close friend 37	Change in residence 20
Prison time or institution 63	Change in line of work 36	Change of school 20
Death of a family member 63	Change in number of arguments (more or less) 35	Increase or decrease in recreation 19
Personal injury or illness 53	Taking on a mortgage or loan 30	Increase or decrease in church activity 19

Instructions: Circle the totals of the life events you have experienced over the previous year. Total them at the bottom.

Marriage 50	Change in work responsibilities (promotion or demotion) 29	Increase or decrease in social activity 18
Being fired at work 47	Child leaving home 29	Taking on a loan 17
Marriage or relationship reconciliation 45	In-law troubles 29	Major change in sleep habits 16
Retirement 45	Outstanding personal achievement 28	Increase family gatherings 15
Major health or behavior change in a family member 44	Spouse beginning or ceasing work 26	Change in eating habits (more or less) 15
Pregnancy 40	Beginning or ceasing formal schooling 26	Vacation 13
Sexual difficulties 39	Major change in living condition (renovation, remodeling, construction) 25	Major holidays 12
Addition of a family member (birth, adoption, parent care, etc.) 39	Revision in personal habits (positive or negative) 24	Minor violations of the law (traffic tickets, speeding, etc.) 11

Total:

Identify whether you are:

- Below 150: low susceptibility to health breakdown.
- 150–300: 50% susceptibility to health breakdown.
- 300 or higher: 80% or greater likelihood of health breakdown.

This is not a crystal ball, but rather a predictive index that should act as a sign, something to make you think. Welcome to wake-up call number 1. You are either earning your health or earning your illness; the choice is up to you.

Sign 2 of a Life in Default: You're Living in Fake Health

As I rolled over in my bed and hit my alarm clock, I peered out the window to see if the sun was up yet. Nope. I shifted my body to get out of bed. Every joint in my body hurt. My low back ached, my neck was stiff, and to move my shoulders was painful. I had finally fallen asleep just four hours before and already it was time to wake up. As I got up and went to the bathroom to wash my face, I felt the familiar scratching in my throat. A telltale sign that I was about to get sick.

As I walked into the kitchen to make my morning shake I felt the bloating starting again. I had not even eaten anything yet. No matter what I ate lately, there would be this constant bloating that would not go away. Persistently, I kept pushing through because anything less would be a quitter's mentality. I got down to the gym exhausted with zero energy to start my workout, and as soon as I entered the gym, I realized I had walked by my water bottle, workout program, and towel. I had laid them out on the table next to the door the night before specifically so I wouldn't forget. My stress cup was overflowing and I had so many signs, but simply ignored them because I figured it was what was required for success.

This had been my cycle for about four years. Every three months I was due for a really good cold, which would be followed by a sinus infection, while the only constant was energy loss and brain fog. I was living in the fake health continuum, and chances are good that so are you. Welcome to sign number 2 of a life in default, shown in Figure 3.1.

A Closer Look at the Fake Health Continuum

On the far left side, you have death and disease. It is exactly what it sounds like. This is where the inner disease has become so great, that the window for prevention has closed and there has been a break in the system. Your health is

FAKE HEALTH CONTINUUM

Figure 3.1   The fake health continuum.

Source: OWN IT Coaching / Justin Roethlingshoefer.

bankrupt, and the medical system now has to treat your diabetes, heart disease, heart attack, stroke, dementia, or some other type of chronic illness. You are now forced to prioritize your illness. Going back and forth between medical facilities, seeing different doctors and specialists, getting admitted for treatment or surgery simply to try and get you back into the fake health hole.

On the far right side, you have true health. This is a place of abundance, and although it may look slightly different for everyone, it reflects something like this. You wake up in the morning full of energy, popping out of bed. You get your gym clothes that you laid out the night before, kiss your spouse, and run out the door to the gym even without the morning coffee. You get an energetic sweat in, finish the rest of your morning routine, and come home ready to get the kids off to school. You sit down behind your desk with an overwhelming clarity getting everything done on your to-do list for the day. Powering through meetings with authority, guiding and directing with confidence, and feeling like you are driving the day and not having the day drive you. The same energy you started your day with carries you through evening soccer practice with the kids or that social event you needed to attend for your business, only to come home at night, connect with your spouse, put your head on your pillow, and sleep deeply. Ready to repeat it all again the next day, you think life is working.

Then there is this large spectrum in the middle. Fake health:

Disease free, but symptom full.

Let that sink in for a second.

The place where your cup is overflowing from stress, but
you choose to ignore it.

The place where your body is writing checks that it
doesn't have the capital to cash.

The place your rhythm is all out of whack.

In fake health, you suffer from unknown weight gain,
exhaustion, brain fog, irritability, bloating, anxiety, lack of
focus, low energy, body aches, insomnia, low libido, headaches, and overwhelm. Just to name a few. However you are
told all these things are normal.

That is what it takes to run a business.

That is what it requires to be an entrepreneur.

That is what leadership looks like.

That's what happens when you have kids.

This is what you are signing up for when you get married.

That is what 40 looks like.

That is just a male or female thing.

ALL LIES. All narratives that keep you in the state of fake
health. The sad thing about it is that the smaller your window
gets for you to be proactive and make your way into true health,
until one day, it seems like overnight, the window slams shut
and throws you unexpectedly into death and disease. Your
wake-up call. The dysfunction you accepted as normal has
become a mess, and now you are forced to prioritize it, and try
to clean it up. Life has to stop. Those whom depend on you are
now forced to care for you. Those whom you are leading now
don't have a leader.

A Dangerous Cycle

There are more consequences than being made fun of at wedding dances for not being able to find the rhythm, and it comes at the expense of our life. There is a cycle that occurs in the fake health continuum that quickly builds momentum:

- Your body can't dissociate mental, physical, spiritual, and emotional stress leading to chronic overreaching.
- Chronic overreaching in any combination creates chronic stress.
- Chronic stress creates chronic inflammation.[2]
- Chronic inflammation creates chronic symptoms—symptoms you deem as normal.
- Chronic symptoms create chronic illness.
- Chronic illness is the leading cause of death, killing 71% of Americans.[3]

The leading cause of death in the United States is earned. Earned because of a life in default.

You did not go to bed one night and wake up with diabetes.

You did not go to bed one night and wake up 40 pounds overweight.

You did not go to bed one night and wake up with heart disease.

You did not go to bed one night and wake up with Alzheimer's.

You did not go to bed one night and wake up with cancer.

You either earn your illness or you earn your health.

I need your wake-up call not to be a disease, but rather this chapter. I need you to begin to understand the language of your body so that you can begin to live differently and make a change. You know you don't feel well. You know you don't feel optimal. You know there are habits that need to be cleaned up. You just don't know what it is costing you.

If you are not earning your health, you are earning your illness. It is time to get honest with yourself on what symptoms you have been accepting as normal. What signs your body has been trying to communicate to you. That whisper of "I need something to change" is not a voice to be feared or ignored, but rather one to be thankful for. The longer you ignore it, the further down the fake health continuum you get. As speaker and author Ed Mylett talks about in *The Power of One More*, what if your opportunity for one more came earlier than it should have because of a failure to live differently? Wouldn't it be a shame if it was 20 or 30 years earlier than it should have been like those 14 people the pastor spoke about earlier?

Fake health has become normal. I am calling you to be different.

Sign 3 of a Life in Default: You Have Missed the Island

I was keynoting at a business leader passive income event in Austin, Texas, when I first told this story. I was not sure how it would land, but as I got off stage, I was bombarded by about 40 people all wanting to understand how to get off the island they suddenly were made aware they were living on. It is far too common to go through life head down, working hard, finding success in multiple areas, but fail to lift your head up and see where you actually are, and not sure how you go there.

The story went like this. There was a young man who had a dream. He was on a journey to execute on his passion and influence the world. He watched himself from 30,000 feet as if he were watching a game piece move on a Monopoly game board. A sense of pride filled the young man as he watched the dream version of him energetically moving from milestone to milestone before he slowed down at one location.

Trying to keep moving himself forward, he reached down but he couldn't touch his dreamlike body. As he took a look closer he saw where the dream version of him had stopped. "Welcome to Sacrifice Town" the sign read. Here, you will have everything you need. You will find business success and financial success. You will have a great family, live in a great home, and not want for anything. But it is the place where all your success came at the direct expense of something else. It meant sacrificing quality sleep to send emails until 10 and 11 o'clock at night. Tossing and turning because you couldn't stop thinking about that meeting. Missing out on your kids' soccer games, family gatherings, and dance recitals because you were busy with clients. Never getting into a healthy rhythm because business travel just made it impossible. Forgoing family dinners to take business dinners, and skipping the gym because you needed to get to the office. The longer the young man watched himself stay there, the slower his dream self-started to move, until he fell down a deep, dark hole.

Waking up in a panic, the young man got up, washed his face, before laying back down to go back to sleep. As he went back into dreamland he found himself in a similar position. There was great pride and enthusiasm seeing himself succeed financially and make an impact in a powerful way, but again, the dream version of himself was stuck in one place. This time the sign read "Welcome to Averageville." Here, you again find great success in all areas of your life, but if you were to be honest with yourself from a health standpoint, you are just average. You are just like the average American. You are on track to have a lifespan that is 25% less than every other developed country in the world, while relying on 10 times the health expenditure. You use medication prescribed by the doctor to control blood pressure, cholesterol, and stress, while always telling yourself tomorrow will be a good day to try something different. You get out of the shower each morning and the person you see in the mirror looks less and less like the person that you once knew. Anything athletic or fitness-related you talk about are the glory days and how you used to be stronger or be able to run faster. You see yourself as different, but if you were to be honest your habits, behaviors, and pursuit of success have landed you in a fake health position just the same as the average American. The longer he watched himself, the slower he started to move and it got to a point where he wasn't even sure if it was him anymore until he fell down a deep, dark hole.

As he woke up covered in sweat, he grabbed his stomach and face to make sure he wasn't the person he saw in the dream. Bothered and slightly fearful to go back to sleep in regards to what he might see this time, he rolled over to the cold part of the bed. Slowly he drifted back to sleep, arriving back to the same game board. This time, however, the dream version of himself was moving with energy that never seemed to stop.

Really hoping there was a sign that told him where he was, he took a closer look. The sign read, "Welcome to Abundance Island." The place where there is more than enough time, energy, and resources to have your health and your success. You still have the financial and business success, but it did not require sacrificing your health. Mentally, physically, spiritually, and emotionally you are whole, enjoying the fruit in your life. You have found the rhythm. There are true seasons of stress and overreaching, but they are met with recovery and regeneration. Life is working. You are mentally clear. You take on stress, but then execute to relieve it. You are fit. You get quality time with your family. There is more than enough time to get everything done, while your energy is on auto renewal.

As the young man looked around him, he saw a tall bearded man dressed in white, and he asked, "What was the secret the third man knew that the first two didn't?"

Very calmly and lovingly he looked over at the young man and said, "There is no secret. Abundance Island is available to everyone. It is how life is designed. It is simply a decision of whether you want to walk over the bridge and live intentionally or not." As the young man was about to ask another question, the bearded man smiled and put his hand to his mouth, whispering, "It is already prepared for you, but you have to prepare yourself."

You see, the young man's dream is each one of our reality. We are in one of three places: Sacrifice Town, Average-ville, or Abundance Island. There is no argument as to where we want to be, just like there is no argument that we want to be in true health. Both Abundance Island and true health have been prepared for each one of you, but it requires intentional preparation and a life by design in order to find yourself there.

It doesn't happen by accident. There is no secret code. It is not an exclusive club. It doesn't even have a guard at the gate. In fact, you just have to decide if you want to live differently.

This is not like a game of Plinko, where you cascade down a board and end up where you do by luck. This is 100% an outcome based on intention and design.

> What is your Life Stress Score according to the Holmes and Rahe scale?
>
> What symptoms are you suffering from?
>
> Are you in fake health?
>
> What place are you living in?
>
> Why has it taken you until now to be honest with yourself?

4

The Solution: Heart Rate Variability

"Once people take ownership over the decision to receive feedback, they're less defensive about it."

—Adam Grant

WOULDN'T IT BE amazing if there was a way to understand how your body was adapting to the stress and strain you were placing it under? A way to understand if the mental, emotional, spiritual, and physical stress you are overreaching with is in proper rhythm with the habits, behaviors, and lifestyle choices you were regenerating with? Well, I have good news: there is. It is your solution to a life by default, and one of the most holistically integrated languages your body has to show you quantifiably how you are adapting to mental, physical, spiritual, and emotional stress. It's called heart rate variability (HRV); even though technically how many devices measure it is pulse rate variability (PRV), we refer to everything as HRV.[1,2]

Your body has a language, and that language is HRV.

Understanding HRV Basics

Since 2003, I have been measuring HRV, and it was my major focus of study during my postgraduate research. When your heart beats, you would think that it beats at regular intervals, meaning static time segments between beats, but this actually isn't true.[3]

Let's take someone, for example, who has a resting pulse rate of 60 beats per minute. Math would tell you that this person's heart is beating at 1 beat per second (60 beats divided by 60 seconds is 1 beat per second). But that is not how our body operates. The time intervals between beats vary by milliseconds (ms). When you are adapting to stress really well and your parasympathetic (rest, digest, relax) nervous system is in proper rhythm between overreaching and regeneration, there will be a high amount of variability between beats. Maybe 700 ms, 795 ms, 822 ms, 710 ms, and so on. See Figure 4.1 for an example of what this looks like.

I like to draw the analogy that your heart beats like that wavy windsock man you see fluttering outside used car dealerships . . . very random, sporadic, and loosey-goosey. This is a sign that your body is adapting to the stress very well.

On the other hand, when you are not adapting to stress as well or there is a heavy season of overreaching and the rhythm is off, your sympathetic (fight, flight, stress) nervous system is dominant, and there will be a low amount of variability between beats. Maybe something like 720 ms, 750 ms, 745 ms, 760 ms, and so on. It is much more rhythmic and static.

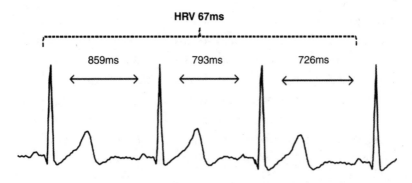

HEART RATE VARIABILITY IS DETERMINED BY THE
TIME BETWEEN HEART BEATS, KNOWN AS RR
INTERVALS.

Figure 4.1 **Heart rate variability.**
© *John Wiley & Sons, Inc.*

What explains this difference? The reason is your brain's main job is to keep you alive, and since we all still have a primitive brain that has hypersensitivity to stress, when your brain experiences any form of stress, real or perceived, mental, physical, spiritual, or emotional, positive or negative, your brain's reaction is: "something is coming to kill you, a bear, wildebeest, person or something else; I have to keep you alive." That is its only goal. And thus, it begins to regulate the beats and activate the sympathetic nervous system.

It is very easy to see how this system could become chronically overactive if you were not aware of it or lived a life by default. The interesting part is when you look at morning HRV trends for a variety of people, downward trends are not caused by a single thing. If you took five different people and the previous day one had run a marathon, the other got in an intense fight with a spouse throughout the evening, another had to make a series of very difficult business decisions, another was going through anxiety and depression, and another was changing careers, the curves would look the same: a decreasing trendline because the body doesn't know the difference among mental, physical, spiritual, or emotional stressors. For the first time, you are now aware of a metric to help guide you and understand your body's adaptation, based on habits and lifestyle choices.

By looking at all the research I would argue that if you can:

- Keep a steady blood glucose (measure and generate awareness 1 week– month a year).
- Minimize micronutrient deficiency (get tested cellularly 2–4× a year).
- Maximize oxygen efficiency (measure VO_2 max 2–4× a year).
- Maximize sleep quality (measure quality on a nightly basis).

You will be able to minimize unnecessary stress on your body and reduce the majority of chronic illnesses. The greatest part about this is that HRV is influenced by each one of those, which makes it the single greatest biometric for awareness we currently have.

In general, you want to see your HRV rising. If on a weekly, monthly, or three-month trend, you see it going up, it means you are adapting well to the stressors you are placing on yourselves and are in a good rhythm between overreaching and regeneration. On the other hand, if on a weekly, monthly, or three-month trend, you see it going down, it means you are not adapting well to the stressors and are out of rhythm. It can act as an awareness alert to say you need to replace some overreaching behaviors with something more regenerative. It could be focusing on sleep, hydrating differently, meditating, breathwork, or simply getting outside and getting in a different environment.

An Increase in HRV Studies

HRV is one of the metrics that has become increasingly popular over the last several years with research articles exponentially increasing almost 100 times since 2016. The problem, however, is that HRV is usually misused and misunderstood, especially within the health and wellness industry. This is why we need to empower you.

HRV is simply communication. It is your body communicating how it is adapting to stress and strain. If you have a low HRV for a single day, it does not mean you are going to die, or even something is wrong. In fact, until you get about 7–10 days' worth of data, it is hard to understand what it actually means for you. You need to see the trends. In general, higher is better. It represents a greater capacity to take on stress, and a more effective ability to cope with it internally. Think of a bigger cup with more holes. High HRV is associated with healthy conditions and decreased likelihood of chronic illness conditions,[4] while low HRV is associated with diseased conditions. In fact, one meta-analysis study looked at a total of 32 different white papers with over 38,000 participants and found that lower HRV parameter values were significant predictors of higher all-cause mortality rates and a great predictor of chronic illness across different healthy ages, sex, continents, populations, and recording lengths.[5,6]

This is incredibly significant because it confirms that a single metric is available to provide you with insight and gain awareness of the impact of your daily habits and behaviors on your long-term health. If you are not measuring HRV and understanding what behaviors or habits are having the greatest impact, then you are choosing to give away your power, live in default, and earn your future illness.

Introducing the Four Pillars of Ownership

There are several types of factors that impact HRV:[7]

- Pathological
- Physiological
- Psychological
- Environmental
- Lifestyle
- Genetic

What we have been able to do is break down these factors into actionable practices that you can take ownership of in order to have a personalized system based on what works for you, while using HRV as a guiding tool. These factors are what we call the four pillars of ownership:

- Fuel
- Build
- Renew
- Repair

When building a life by design on your true health journey, one of these pillars will need to be focused on at a time. Within each one of these four pillars, there are two foundational principles with baseline habits that help build your design, while HRV provides insight as to which habits are working for you or against you.

1—Fuel	2—Build	3—Repair	4—Renew
A—Nutrition	A—Training and Movement	A—Sleep	A—Self Care
B—Hydration	B—Mindset	B—Immune Response	B—Environment

For example, we had two clients come to us who were suffering from severe lack of energy, both being in the health and wellness industry. They were getting sick more often, were not sleeping well, and overall just frustrated. We had one of them start intermittent fasting and the other stop, and the result for both was an increase in HRV, energy, weight loss immune function, and sleep. It was simply a shift in stress load and helping them re-establish a better rhythm based on the season of life. In Chapters 5–8, we get very specific as to what the pillars mean to you and how you can implement them based on your uniqueness and lifestyle.

HRV as Your Starting Point for Everything

Being from Edmonton, our claim to fame is that we are home to the biggest mall in North America, West Edmonton Mall, and 14th biggest in the world. I went home last Christmas and went to the mall for the first time in about

10 years. It had grown massively and expanded with four more phases and an entire new floor. It has an amusement park, water park, underground submarine, go-karts, Sea-World, zoo, and all the typical shops and restaurants.

As I parked my car, I looked up and took notice of the area around me. "D3" was on a big green sign right outside the water park. I made a note so I could get back to my car and went inside. As I crossed off the last item on my Christmas shopping list, I headed in the direction of what I thought was the water park. Where I had parked my vehicle. After about five minutes there were stores I didn't recognize and I began to realize I didn't know where I was going. I stopped someone who seemed to know exactly where they were going and said, "Excuse me, do you know where the parking lot D3 is? It's a big green sign by the water park."

They responded, "Yes, go up the escalator to the next floor and take a right."

I followed those directions, got up to the top of the escalator, took a right and proceeded to walk around for another three minutes, finding myself in the same predicament. Walking aimlessly, unsure of where to go. I proceeded to ask someone else who seemed to know where they were going. I asked, "Excuse me, do you know where the parking lot D3 is? It's a big green sign by the water park."

They responded, "Yes, you need to go back to that escalator and take a left."

A simple mistake I figured, and so I proceeded back to the escalator and took the left but nothing seemed familiar. After five more minutes of walking, I stopped at the mall directory. As I looked at the directory, I immediately found the water park and the parking lot labeled D3 in green, but that was not enough. It was not until I found the big red dot that said "you are here" that I was able to begin help-ing myself.

It is just like your health. The red dot "you are here" is your HRV. You know where you want to go, know how you want to feel, look, and think like, but you have been acting without knowing where you are. You ask people around you who seem to be on the right track, look the part, or seem confident in where they are going, but in actuality, all they know is what works for them. When you skip the learning, educating, and understanding process, you will find yourself lost, giving away your power to those who are not motivated to help you. A life by design knows where your little red dot is and can build a plan that is personalized, curated, and actionable to where we want to go.

You were built to be different, so you live differently. The habits and behaviors of others may work for them, but they may actually be hurting you. It's time to learn the lan-guage of your body.

Tools for Measuring HRV

"What should my HRV be?" I hear the question all the time, and it's a trick question. There's not an "optimal" HRV for men, women, or even a certain age group. HRV is a highly individualized metric that varies from person to person, which is why it is so powerful for personalization. You should compare yourself to you and only you. By living your life that way, you will begin to see how your body is adapting.

I used to be a purist and only get data from the purest source, which is a heart rate monitor with a chest strap or an actual EKG, but as you can imagine that would be extremely unsustainable. You would have to wear a heart rate strap all day long, remember to collect your data first thing in the morning, or have access to an EKG machine. That was my chosen option since I was 14 and obsessed with this type of data, but what I have learned working with thousands of people is that you need something simple and easy to get passive measurements in order for it to be sustainable and empowering. To do this, I recommend two wearable devices the most often. WHOOP and Oura are best in class for a few reasons:

- Scientific validity
- Ease of use and passive data collection
- Reliability and consistency

Are they perfect? Absolutely not. Do they provide the data that we can build on to help you understand how your habits and behaviors are impacting you? Absolutely. The way you choose which one you want is simple. Do you like to wear a ring or a wrist band more? Oura is a ring, and WHOOP is a wrist band.

Looking at HRV Ranges

As much as HRV is a personalized metric and should not be compared, I wanted to provide you with a reference range based on the data of millions of people.

No matter what device you have—Apple, Garmin, Fitbit, Polar, or something else—you can look at your HRV trend and compare it to the reference range in the following figures to provide another wake-up call. If you are lower than the norms or in the lower percentiles, and have a stagnant or downward trend in your own data, your body is trying to communicate something to you. The question is what are you going to do about it? Keep your head in the sand or begin to live differently?

Figure 4.2 shows the middle 50% of HRV values by age.[8] Figure 4.3 shows another view.

Again, the reason I show these to you is not so you can compare yourself to someone else, but to give you a reference range to better understand what your current normal has provided you.

HRV has been shown to be a great predictor of biological age.[9,10] That's a measure of how your body is aging internally

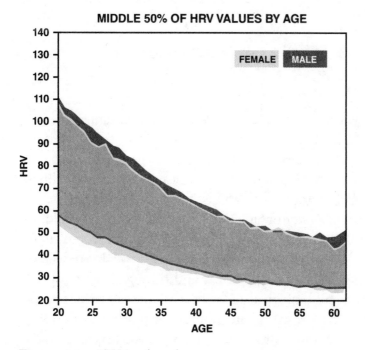

Figure 4.2   HRV values by age.

© *John Wiley & Sons, Inc.*

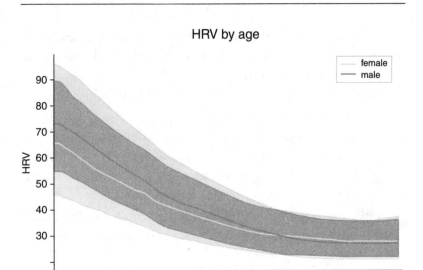

Figure 4.3   Another view of HRV by age.

© *John Wiley & Sons, Inc.*

versus your chronological age, which is the number of birth-days you have experienced. The intent is to maintain a low biological age versus our chronological age as it is a key con-tributor to making sure we are resistant to chronic illness, stress, and a variety of all-cause mortality circumstances.

We had a client come through who was 51 years old. He thought he was in great health, but was having some energy issues, and wasn't sleeping well. When we looked at his HRV he had an average of 21, and through a series of test-ing, found his biological age to be 67. Now as we went deeper with this client, we began to discover that he was on high blood pressure medication, anxiety medication, and had been diagnosed as a pre-diabetic. Here is what makes this story worth telling and why it applies to everyone reading this book. He did not believe he was unhealthy until he saw how low his HRV was and how it impacted his biological age. The high blood pressure medication, anxiety and pre-diabetes diagnosis were simply normal to him, and since there was no impact on his day-to-day activities, none of those served as his wake-up call. These metrics were his wake-up call.

Fast-forward 10 months after instituting purposeful behavior change through the four pillars of ownership and personalized testing: he was able to triple his HRV to 64 and see a decrease in biological age to 49, less than what his chronological age was.

I want you to take a second and reflect on the Chapter 3 signs of default and reflect on what your body is communicating to you through HRV. You have been so busy lying to yourself that you don't even recognize what is true anymore. Data doesn't lie. It has no feeling, bias, or emotion. Just the pure truth that, when used the right way, can be the wake-up call you need to get honest with yourself and empower you back to a life by design.

What is your HRV number?

What is your body trying to communicate to you?

PART

II

The Four Pillars of Ownership

5

Pillar 1: Fuel

"Food is your body's fuel. Without fuel, your body wants to shut down."

—Ken Hill

Now THAT YOU have the awareness of the rhythm your body is currently operating in, you are going to dive into the actions that you will eventually build your life by design with. As we go through each of these pillars in this chapter and Chapters 6–8, there will be some habits that will work for you, and some that won't. There will be some that are right for the season of life stress you are in and some that won't. This is why you will use your data to determine your own personalized life by design and live differently than someone else who reads the same book as you. Remember, we are helping you build your system, not fitting you into everyone else's.

When it comes to taking ownership of your health, fuel is the first pillar. Fuel is what anything needs to get going. The fuel could be gas for a car or batteries for different electronics. It could be ink for a pen. The fuel type changes, but the concept remains the same. Your body is no different. If you have too much or too little fuel, it is a stressor on your body and something that it has to adapt to. If you put the wrong fuel in your body you can break down. If you need a metaphor to understand that, then try putting diesel in a gas tank and see how far you get. That is one expensive mistake, just like putting the wrong fuel into your body.

The two foundations for the pillar of fuel are nutrition and hydration, as you find out in this chapter, but understanding those is not as easy as you may think. You need to ensure the habits are seen from the perspective of stress and how the behaviors you engage in are either turning the stress faucet on higher or poking another hole as a stress reliever.

Foundational principle 1—Nutrition

You are told to avoid salt, eat fewer eggs, eat less red meat, don't cook with butter, cook with refined oils, eat fancy packaged foods, but yet you continue to keep getting sick, feel lethargic, and watch your health decline.

Nutrition has become overcomplicated. Everyone has their opinion, and every week it seems there is a new marketing gimmick trying to get you to take on a new diet. There is more conflicting misinformation out there than ever before, while concepts that were held up as truths only turn up as lies. In the domain of nutrition, I want you to come back to simplicity. Habits that are sustainable and create real change. With many of the nutrition foundational habits, you'll notice there is some overlap with some of the foundations of other pillars and you can stack them together for efficiency. Remember, we are controlling what you can control. For example, taking a five-minute walk after a meal is a baseline habit in both nutrition, and training and movement. Being able to adopt one of those habits is double-dipping and will increase your speed in understanding if the habit is right for you.

The following sections cover different aspects of improving your nutrition: timing, portion size, food order, tools, and testing.

Timing When You Eat

When we think about timing, everyone talks about intermittent fasting. You have to remember, however, it is a stressor. I have seen so many people starving themselves and pushing that fasting window longer and longer, only to eat more calories in a condensed amount of time, and continue to eat late into the night, impacting the quality of sleep they are supposedly striving for. A perfect example of how something the world tells you is healthy may actually be hurting you.

I am a fan of intermittent fasting or time-restricted eating. The data and evidence are incredibly positive when it comes to health benefits. ranging from cellular regeneration to immune function optimization to weight loss, but we have to remember it isn't for all people all the time. And it is definitely not something to compete with to see who can push their windows the longest. The first nutrition habit I want to touch on is stopping eating three hours before bed and not eating for three hours after waking. This serves two purposes.

- By adding the three hours before bed, with a 6- to 9-hour sleeping window, and 3 hours after waking, you have automatically created a 12–15-hour fasting window, without even trying, while maximizing your ability to get quality sleep.
- It empowers you to create a separation of time between waking and eating to focus on hydration first thing in the morning, to minimize cravings and energy fluctuation throughout the day. (Find out more about hydration later in this chapter.)

Choosing the Right Portion Size

After adding in a restricted eating window, the next habit to focus on is portion size. The portions have become outrageous in the United States, and thus cause a major stressor on your body to break down the amount of food you could consume on a meal-by-meal basis. You want to make sure you don't have more than one serving size of protein, carbs, fats, and veggies at each meal.

One serving of each looks like this:

- Protein—size of your palm
- Fats—size of your thumb
- Carbs—size of a cupped hand that is leveled off
- Veggies—size of your fist

When focused on these portion sizes it leads to another 3-2-1 rule that makes it easy to remember and implement:

- 3 meals a day (1 portion size of each per meal: protein, fats, carbs, and veggies)

- 2 pieces of fruit with a protein source per day
- 1 big salad with a protein source (could be one of the meals)

This rule eliminates any tracking of calories and macros that can lead to disordered eating and obsessive focus, which is a mental and emotional stressor that your body has to adapt to, but also is not sustainable. The U.S. Food and Drug Administration tells you that 0.36 grams of protein for every pound of body weight is acceptable,[1] but I need you to hear that the goal should be 1 gram of protein per pound of body weight.[2] By following the 3-2-1 rule, you can hit that target, which will have a big impact on your feelings of hunger and insatiability. Carbs are like the kindling for the energy fire, but protein are the logs. We need more logs to really enhance the energy burn all day long.

As you read this you may be thinking, "I know this. I need something sexier!" The question is, "you may know it, but are you doing it consistently." This is a trend you will notice in some of the other pillars. Remember, the people winning in their health don't do anything extraordinary; they do the ordinary things with extraordinary intention and consistency.

Eating Food in the Proper Order

Another thing you can begin to focus on is food order. Regulating blood sugar is essential when it comes to health and longevity. The use of blood glucose monitors (see the next section) has really allowed us to see how food order, food type, meal timing, and movement impact your blood glucose levels. In fact, I will be bold enough to say if you were to track blood glucose and HRV (see heart rate variability in Chapter 4), and build a life by design around optimizing those two metrics you could eradicate 99% of chronic illness we suffer from today.[3,4]

There is a woman on Instagram called Glucose Goddess who does a great job highlighting some of the small changes you can make to generate blood glucose stability, and she is definitely worth following. But what she has demonstrated and what several studies have also validated is that eating veggies first, proteins and fats second, and carbohydrates third allows blood glucose spikes to minimize by about 75%, keeping blood sugar much more regulated and allowing you to feel satiated longer. The other thing that has been shown to decrease the blood sugar spike is a five-minute walk after any meal (see Chapter 6 for more details).

Using Tools for Tracking

Often you need a tool or test to bring a heightened level of awareness and personalization once you have put a solid foundation of habits and behaviors in place. I love the continuous glucose monitor (CGM) as a tool to help educate you in real time, and understand the internal impact of food you are eating and other habits from the Fuel pillar.

When you are in alignment with what your body needs nutritionally, you will notice HRV rise daily due to the decrease in internal stress, and can be affirmed with a CGM and blood testing. Notice there is no macro counting, no calorie counting, no set diet like paleo or keto, but rather a framework that empowers you to have flexibility while holding you accountable. Nutrition does not have to be a struggle. It needs to be simple. When looking at food quality, HRV is a great way to see how food timing and what you eat impact your body.

Here's an example: Cody struggled for a long time with his nutrition. He was gluten-free, lactose-free, followed intermittent fasting, and tried to follow the paleo regime, but constantly found himself exhausted and adding weight. He found himself eating all the packaged paleo foods because they were convenient, and only ate from 4–10 p.m. When we looked at his HRV, it was 21 and his blood glucose went through extreme peaks and valleys. If you asked anyone, they would say he is "doing everything right," but in fact he was not doing what was right for him. Over eight weeks, we had him shift to the 3-2-1 rule, had him eat between 10 a.m. and 6 p.m., and had him focused primarily on portion size. His HRV jumped to 49 and his blood glucose variation was almost indistinguishable. His energy was back, his brain fog was gone, and the mental stress he was feeling diminished.

This is why you need to identify what habits are right for you, and bring awareness to the actions with HRV. If you were to follow each habit in this chapter but all your food choices were deep fried, processed, and full of sugar, you would notice your HRV start to drop. A wake-up call. On the other hand, if you were to focus on whole, nonprocessed foods, you would begin to see an increase in HRV. We all know the idea behind the grocery store. When you go in, the area that you want to shop from is the perimeter. It has your fruits and vegetables, meats, eggs, dairy, quality carbohydrates, and all the middle aisles contain your processed, sugar-laden foods. The more focused on whole, nonprocessed foods you can be, the better.

Getting the Right Tests

When it comes to further optimization, blood testing is another great tool to understand what is happening inside your body and how the food you are eating is being broken down and used. There are two types of blood testing you want to be conscious of:

- blood serum testing
- cellular blood testing

The blood serum testing is what you are likely used to. It's what the doctors are doing during your annual visits. Complete metabolic panels, complete blood counts, and cardiovascular lipid panels. These are important blood draws to see organ function and how the body is operating. Biomarkers like hemoglobin A1c, fasting glucose, lipoprotein (a), and apolipoprotein B are all key biomarkers that can give us more information on how your nutritional habits are cultivating outcomes within your body, and if you are on your way to earning health or illness.

Cellular testing, however, is looking inside the cell. It tells you what micronutrients are getting from the serum into the cell, and what your body is actually deficient in.[5] It becomes pretty obvious why cellular testing is so critical, but yet, it is never done. It is critical for two reasons:

- Micronutrient deficiencies cause internal stress and disease.
- Targeted repletion is the solution.

Micronutrients are the vitamins, minerals, antioxidants, and chemicals in our bodies that are used to perform every biological function necessary to survive and thrive. If you become deficient, your body believes that you do not have any of the raw material, vitamins, or minerals to use, and due to that, you get tired, fatigued, and sick. A great example of this is that you could have adequate magnesium in your blood serum testing, but when a cellular test is done there are functional deficiencies, meaning it is not getting from the serum into the cell for use. Magnesium is used for over 300 metabolic processes in the body so you can see the issue here. By continuing on this way, you would develop a chronic micronutrient deficiency, causing more stress on the body and manifesting in the formation of chronic illness.[6]

Remember, the cumulative effects of cellular micronutrient dysfunction are disease, fatigue, and pain.

The cumulative effects of optimal cell function are health, vigor, and energy.

By looking at cellular micronutrient testing, our team at OWN IT formulates custom supplementation that is built for you based on the functional deficiencies, so that there are custom therapeutic doses to replenish what is not only missing in the cell, but also solve for the reason why. By getting the cellular testing done every three to six months, you can see the changes and how your body has adapted and what needs to be reformulated to continue to combat cellular micronutrient dysfunction. That is a life by design.

Another test you may have seen storm onto the market is DNA and epigenetic testing. This is not 23andMe or some other heavily marketed DNA test. This needs to be a specific test targeting certain gene sequencing to ensure you are getting quality data when it comes to predispositions. DNA and epigenetic testing allows you to understand what you are predisposed to. It is not a crystal ball or a death sentence, but is powerful information that can further refine your buy-in and authority over the habits that we discussed earlier. When you can attach your literal genetic makeup as to why certain habits matter for you, your buy-in to those habits significantly increases. There is a direct correlation to buy-in and your level of consistency, which in this case will lead to an increase in HRV, which further perpetuates your desire to be consistent with the habit. Do you see the positive feedback loop here?

When you think about DNA and epigenetics, there are a few important notes. Your DNA is what is passed on from your family lineage based on what you are predisposed to, but epigenetics act like light switches that turn on or off aspects of our genetic code.[7] Your behaviors and environment influence the epigenetics. This is why someone who has diabetes run in their family and is genetically predisposed to high blood glucose and insulin sensitivity may never get diabetes. The epigenetics based on how someone is living ultimately determines that.

Think about it like this. Let's put two people on a ski hill. One person is genetically predisposed to high blood glucose and insulin sensitivity while another person is not. The genetically predisposed person is placed halfway down the ski hill; the other person starts at the top of the ski hill. They both go down the hill at the same speed, meaning they engage in the same behaviors, poor eating habits, lack of exercise, and high stress levels. Who hits the bottom first and realizes diabetes? The person who started halfway down with the predisposition, of course, but the person who was not predisposed ended up getting diabetes as well because of their habits.

On the other hand, if the person who was genetically predisposed had awareness and changed their behaviors to focus on high-quality eating habits like we talked about earlier, was fit and built a strong foundation of fitness while placing high value on managing their stress through sleep and self-care, basically living a life by design, they would go down the hill very slowly. Going through cut backs, hitting chair lifts, taking them higher up the mountain, and actually never get diabetes, where still the first person who wasn't genetically predisposed would get the diabetes diagnosis because they zoomed down the hill with bad habits.

DNA testing provides such a quality insight to where genetic breaks occur and how we can supplement, fuel, and live differently. The methylation gene testing is such a great example. If there are DNA breaks in the ability to methylate, meaning the ability to start a reaction that makes a molecule usable in the body, there will be decreases in enzyme function and possible build up in toxicity. For example, methylation converts the toxic amino acid (homocysteine) into a beneficial amino acid (methionine). If your body cannot methylate properly, toxins build up in your bloodstream and will eventually cause disease.[8] This shows up in symptoms like fatigue, weight gain, brain fog, mood changes, and issues with focus. A simple multivitamin that is not methylated or certain beverages and food additives can have severe consequences simply because we are not aware. The only way we are able to make these changes and encourage us along the way is to know through testing.

By understanding the blood biomarkers both at the cellular and serum level while knowing what we are genetically predisposed to, we can further refine nutrition, supplementation, hydration, and exercise to maximize the health results we will be seeing. Your body keeps the score. Your body will tell you the story. As long as you are willing to listen.

A Simple Breakdown of Nutrition Habits, Testing, and Tools

Life by Design habits for nutrition include the following:

- Wait to eat for three hours after waking.
- Complete eating three hours before sleeping.
- Three meals a day (with one portion of protein, carbs, fat, and veggies at each meal).
- Two pieces of fruit with a protein source per day.
- One big salad a day with protein source per day (this can replace one meal).
- Each day, eat 1 gram of protein per pound of body weight.
- Walk for five minutes after every meal.
- Focus on eating food in this order: veggies, protein, fats, carbs to regulate blood glucose.

Enhanced personalized testing to further your ownership journey nutritionally includes the following:

- Cellular micronutrient testing
- DNA
- Gut biome testing

Tools to help with your nutrition include the following:

- Continuous glucose monitor (CGM)

Foundational principle 2—Hydration

Our bodies were designed to be 65% water. Our brain, hearts, and lungs were designed to be made up of almost 80% water.[9]

You would think that if God designed you that way, water must be pretty important.

We had a client who ran her insurance business out of North Dakota. It routinely went down to −40°F for a couple weeks every winter. Her hands would crack, and because it was so cold, she never found herself actually thirsty. She constantly suffered from incredibly bad and frequent headaches, which she was always told was due to being hungry or tired. No matter how much sleep she got or how frequent her meals, the headaches were always there. The doctors wanted to put her on a migraine prescription because it is normal for entrepreneurs to get headaches, but she wanted a different solution. Looking back, she was chronically dehydrated, drinking maybe 40 ounces of water a day, if she was lucky. She was simply unaware, just like you.

It has been shown that 75% of Americans are chronically dehydrated.[10] Your lack of awareness has been causing your body stress and you did not even know it. Instead of filling up your water bottle with water, you have been filling up your body's stress cup, adding to the chronic stress that your body has to pay the price for. Drinking enough water has a significant impact in mitigating the risk of chronic illness, decreasing your biological age, and reducing the risk of premature mortality.[11,12] The following sections help you improve your hydration.

Knowing How Much Water to Consume

It is amazing that something as simple as drinking water has been ignored for so long. Once you become thirsty, it is too late. You need to have the awareness and build the habit of the correct quantity.

HRV is extremely valuable in providing a heads up and alert to when you have failed to get the adequate water intake. This is why the first hydration habit to begin to develop sounds really silly; however, it works. Find a water bottle that you love and has the known amount of ounces on it. I suggest 32–40 ounces as a size. I know it sounds silly, but when you find a water bottle you love, you are more likely to take it with you everywhere and pay more attention to it. The reason for knowing the amount of ounces is so that you can easily know how many times you need to fill it up. It is so easy to overestimate our water consumption when we are only drinking at meals from a glass or finishing a bottle of water we pull from the fridge.

Adding Electrolytes

You need half your body weight in ounces of water per day as a minimum.[13] When you start this hydration habit, many people say, "Well, now I just pee all the time." Which leads us to the next habit. Make sure that your water is not only water. You need more than just water to hydrate yourself properly and absorb it into our cells, which is why you need to put electrolytes in your water, especially first thing in the morning to establish a priming of your cells to absorb water throughout the day.[14]

By doing this, the pH of our blood can be regulated, fluid balance can be maintained, and our body's day-to-day functions can be optimized. Magnesium, chloride, potassium, and sodium are the major four electrolytes you need to add to your water in high concentration to make sure that you are creating the optimal concentration gradient.[15] I am a big fan of two different products: LMNT and Redmond ReLyte.

They both have great concentrations of electrolytes, no sugar, and nothing other than the electrolytes in the package.

A way you can take this a step further is by going back to that cellular blood testing that I talk about earlier in this chapter. This allows you to see the exact electrolytes and their concentration deficiency at the cellular level. Empowering you to further personalize your habits, behaviors, and decisions in pursuit of optimal health.

Timing Your Water Intake

If you find yourself waking up in the middle of the night to pee, try to get 75% of your water intake for the day before 3 p.m. This will help with your sleep quality and limit disruptions.

If you are at a high altitude, you will want to add an extra 30–50 ounces of water per day because at altitude you lose more water due to an increase in respiration rate and decrease in atmospheric pressure.

Remember, half your body weight in ounces is only where you start. Coffee, alcohol, and soda do not count. The reason for this is any caffeinated beverage and alcohol is called a diuretic, which actually increases urination, which increases the speed of dehydration, and thus, nutrient depletion. So any of those beverages cannot be included in the total water consumption for the day.

Hydrating Enough When You're Sweating

The addition of activity and sweating requires more rehydration. There is an easy equation called the "Galpin Equation," developed by Dr. Andy Galpin, professor at California

State University at Fullerton. He found the appropriate intake of water during training or heavy sweating was body weight divided by 30 in ounces every 15–20 minutes. This does not mean you need to be precise every 15–20 minutes, but the total intake over the course of the activity time.

So here's the simple formula:

Body weight in pounds / 30 =
   Number in ounces of water every 15 – 20 minutes[16]

When you begin to hydrate properly, you actually get better at sweating, and sweating has major health implications. It has been shown to decrease illnesses, risk of chronic illness, and symptoms; shorten lengths of colds and flus; detoxify the body; and improve circulation and skin health.[17]

Tracking the Importance of Hydration with HRV

Making sure you are properly hydrated both from a water quantity and water quality standpoint is extremely important for your long-term health. As you age, you lose the internal systems to signal your thirst level. We don't exactly know why that is, but it becomes even more important to develop these habits.

Studies show that you only need to be 1% dehydrated to experience a 5% decrease in cognitive function. A 2% decrease in brain hydration can result in short-term memory loss and trigger physical symptoms like cramping, nausea, increase in blood viscosity, and reaction time.[18] These are all major stressors to the body.

As I mentioned before, alcohol and caffeine play a major role in hydration status. When you pair either of these with the lack of water intake, there are exponential stress responses inside the body due to the increase in dehydration.

When you look at HRV and there is a decrease, one of the key ignored culprits is hydration. Look at the difference in HRV when you drink alcohol versus when you don't; when you limit caffeine intake versus when you don't; and when you take in half your body weight in ounces of water a day versus when you don't.

I have a good story that brings the power of HRV and understanding your body to life. On a Thursday night in Italy, Alyse and I went out and I had my first multi-alcoholic drink day of the trip. I had four margaritas (six drinks for the whole 10-day trip) during a four-hour period. Prior to the night out, however, I:

- Worked out that morning
- Tallied 20k steps
- Fasted until noon
- Ate a great lunch, clean snacks, and a protein-heavy dinner
- Drank close to 120 ounces of water
- Was in the sauna for 20 minutes and dipped in the cold shower
- Took all my supplements and electrolytes

Needless to say it was a very "healthy" day. If you look at my HRV, however, it plummeted to 56. That is a low for the year for me.

The next day, I had the exact same day, with the exception of the alcohol and my HRV shot back up to 105. Check out Figure 5.1 for a closer look.

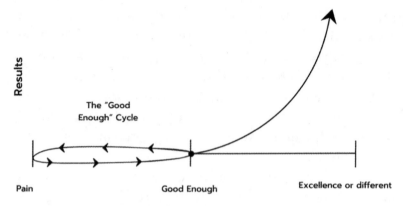

Figure 5.1   A closer look at HRV.

Source: Justin Roethlingshoefer.

I share this story because it highlights how impactful alcohol and hydration are on your system. I used all the tools that people would say are healthy. The sauna, electrolytes, supplements; but the alcohol and dehydration were still extremely stressful on my system and the data showed it. HRV empowers me to make decisions based on what I know the cost is.

It can be pretty scary when you think about the amount of stress you are putting on your body unknowingly. Remember, your bodies are made up of 65% water, and the brain, heart, and lungs, which are key organs in determining maintaining life, are made up of almost 80% water. You were designed to have water be a key part of your daily rhythm; it is time you prioritized it.

A Simple Breakdown of Hydration Habits, Testing, and Tools

Life by Design Habits for hydration include the following:

- Find a water bottle that is at least 20 ounces large that you love! (A bottle that's 32 to 40 ounces is even better.)
- Drink half of your body weight in ounces of water each day. (Pregnant women should take an additional .32 quarts of water. And breastfeeding women should take an additional 1.16 quart of water.)
- Have 20 ounces of water with salt, potassium, magnesium, and chloride each morning to prime your cells (LMNT, Redmond) first thing upon waking.
- Establish a caffeine curfew.

Testing that's worthwhile includes the following:

- CNA
- NIX sweat analysis

Tools to increase your hydration include the following:

- LMNT
- Redmond
- Water bottle

6

Pillar 2: Build

"Take care of your mind, your body will thank you. Take care of your body, your mind will thank you."

—Debbie Hampton

THE GREATEST WAY to handle more stress is to build a stronger foundation. Your mind and body are the two foundations you can build deep and wide to create a bigger cup. Without a strong foundation, there is no way you can generate capacity, create massive impact, and realize the energy in life you desire. This is the pillar where it happens. By focusing on the foundations of training and movement and mindset, you will notice drastic changes in not only HRV (heart rate variability), also but subjectively how you look, think, and feel.

Foundational principle 3—Training and Movement

I want to talk about language here for a minute. This foundation is named training and movement, NOT exercise and movement, for a reason. I was told long ago that exercise is movement without a purpose, where training is done with intention. That is what I want you to embrace. You don't need to be a professional athlete to train. Everybody needs to train their body in order to build the health they desire. Nobody is going to disagree that movement and training are key pillars, and there are tens of thousands of studies validating their importance when it comes to our health, but yet we have still found a way to discount taking action, often again due to confusion and too much choice. There is slow steady-state cardio, high-intensity interval training, group classes, CrossFit, weightlifting, powerlifting, and bodybuilding. Where do you begin and what really matters?

Adding Purpose to Your Movement

It is important to point out that the more specific your goals, the more specific your programming will need to be. If you are striving to be an ironman or professional athlete, the baseline habits we are talking about here don't go away, but you would build on and refine them to increase specificity. That is what makes this journey so awesome. It meets you right where you are. Empowers you to begin to make changes without getting bogged down in the minutiae. From my professional athletes to my most successful entrepreneurs, all have developed their own version of habits into personalized frameworks that establish their life by design. It maximizes their time while optimizing their health. Time is the asset; health is the protective mechanism.

What's the difference between training and movement? I remember when I went from being on my feet all day as a health and performance coach in the NHL, to a more computer-based position as an entrepreneur. There was an adjustment. I would go from working out in the morning, to training players for four hours, to performing massage and manual therapy on players for another couple of hours, only to step onto the ice and direct the rehabbing players before spending the afternoon on the computer getting the next day or week planned. Even though I was only working out once a day, there was a lot of movement in my day. It was not uncommon for me to surpass 25,000 steps each day.

As I went fully into entrepreneurship in 2020, I would still get my daily workout in, but the rest of the day was spent at a desk, catching a flight, driving in cars, or sitting in meetings (a normal, and considered acceptable day). What's interesting is the longer I continued this trend without addressing it, the more my body began to feel off. My hamstrings and low back began to ache. I got more frequent headaches. I didn't feel as good on my runs I took daily; I almost felt stiff, and my HRV average had dropped to 87 compared to my typical average of 102.

It would have been very easy to accept this as my new normal, and this is simply what the life of an entrepreneur and business owner looked like. But we all know by now that is not what a life by design looks like, nor is it what taking ownership of your health looks like, especially when I had a metric looking me square in the eyes telling me exactly what I need to know. So I began to insert habits throughout my day that would increase my energy, address my pains, and additionally change my ability to think clearly. Intentionally, I added two, 10-minute stretch sessions to my day, one mid-morning and one mid-afternoon. I took one meeting a day outside while walking, and during what typically was my time to sit and eat lunch, I added a quick walk with my dog. Those intentional design changes to my day made a major difference. Preventing what would definitely have been health challenges down the road.

When we talk about training, it has to be purposeful exercise. This doesn't mean being distracted. Watching your favorite TV show while on the treadmill, sending text messages during rest intervals, answering emails between sets, all fall under the category of distraction. There was a study that was conducted at Elon University that showed when you engage in distracted exercise the intensity at which you work is significantly lower.[1] The unfortunate reality is this is how the majority of people train. Yet they wonder why showing up and going through the motions is not getting results. The impact of that psychologically and the role it plays in consistency is why people quit.

It's no secret that obesity and weight management are major issues in the United States as 69% of Americans are either overweight or obese, with one-third of the population actually being obese.[2] By adding 150 minutes of purposeful training a week it can not only decrease obesity by 79%, but also reduce the risk of chronic illnesses like diabetes, heart disease, cancer, and stroke by 30%.[3] I would be as bold to say that obesity and being overweight have become normal chronic illnesses in our culture.

Increasing VO$_2$ Max

By tracking or being aware of heart rate during training, we can continue to make sure we are being purposeful with our training. Working this way allows us to do the minimal amount of work for maximal results by developing our VO_2 max, otherwise known as maximum amount of oxygen able to be used at peak output. Now why would that matter to anyone who is not an athlete?

- Because it is the gold standard in helping us understand our level of fitness.
- Because VO_2 max tells us how efficient our body is at carrying oxygen to our brain and muscles. The more efficient we are, the more energy we will have on a daily basis.[4]

In a study conducted with over 120,000 subjects, there was a clear correlation between VO_2 max, HRV, and mortality rate. The higher the VO_2 max, the higher the HRV and the lower the mortality rate,[5] demonstrating how impactful a greater VO_2 max and HRV are to longevity. The goal should be to have as high a VO_2 max number as possible with a target for men above 50 and women above 40.[6]

Table 6.1 shows VO_2 max goals for men by age, and Table 6.2 shows VO_2 max goals for women by age.

By improving your VO_2 max by 1 fitness classification will not only increase your HRV, but also will have a greater influence on longevity than smoking cessation.

The way you increase VO_2 max, and by consequence HRV, can be done a few ways:

- Zone 2 conditioning (which is 60%–70% of your max heart rate)
- Sprinting repeats
- Training for 20 minutes a week at a heart rate above 80% max heart rate

Table 6.1 Goal VO$_2$ max for men by age group. (mL/kg/min).

Fitness Classification	20–24	25–29	30–34	35–39	40–44	45–49	50–54	55–59	60–65
Excellent	>62	>59	>56	>54	>51	>48	>46	>43	>40
Very Good	57–62	54–59	52–56	49–54	47–51	44–48	42–46	40–43	37–40
Good	51–56	49–53	46–51	44–48	42–46	40–43	37–41	35–39	33–36
Average	44–50	43–48	41–45	39–43	36–41	35–39	33–36	31–34	29–32
Fair	38–43	36–42	35–40	33–38	32–35	30–34	29–32	27–30	25–28
Poor	32–37	31–35	29–34	28–32	26–31	25–29	24–27	22–26	21–24
Very Poor	<32	<31	<29	<28	<26	<25	<24	<22	<21

Table 6.2 Goal VO$_2$ max for women by age group (mL/kg/min).

Fitness Classification	20–24	25–29	30–34	35–39	40–44	45–49	50–54	55–59	60–65
Excellent	>51	>49	>46	>44	>41	>38	>36	>33	>30
Very Good	47–51	45–49	43–46	41–44	38–41	36–38	33–36	31–33	28–30
Good	42–46	41–44	38–42	36–40	34–37	32–35	30–32	28–30	25–27
Average	37–41	36–40	34–37	32–35	30–33	28–31	26–29	24–27	22–24
Fair	32–36	31–35	30–33	28–31	26–29	24–27	23–25	21–23	19–21
Poor	27–31	26–30	25–29	24–27	22–25	21–23	19–22	18–20	16–18
Very Poor	<27	<26	<25	<24	<22	<21	<19	<18	<16

105

VO_2 max can be tested a multitude of ways either through an actual metabolic cart (often you need to go into a facility for this), at events that OWN IT hosts, or you can run a mile as quickly as possible, and get an estimated VO_2 max. From this, you can identify your aerobic capacity and find specific heart rate zones to train in so that you can make sure your zone 2 and sprint interval training are going to get the correct adaptation you are looking for.

Planning for Strength Training

We cannot forget the power of strength training. When we strength train, it has another exponential increase in longevity.[7] A recent meta study with over 1.5 million participants showed that strength training as little as three days a week decreased risk of chronic illnesses like cardiovascular disease, cancer, diabetes, lung cancer, and all-cause mortality by 20%. It is such a simple addition to any lifestyle, but the influence on your health is exponential.

The common issue I see with strength training, however, is there is no plan, no target to hit. I am not talking about body fat loss or weight goals. I am talking about measuring certain bodily adaptations to keep you motivated as you learn to love strength training and get more consistent with it.

There are four adaptations in the body that we want to incorporate when thinking about a workout program:

- Muscular strength
- Muscular endurance
- Power production
- Flexibility and mobility

Muscular strength and muscular endurance are different because *strength* has to do with how much weight you can lift, where *endurance* has to do with how long you can do it for. We cannot train both components at the same time so it is critical to be able to know what you need to focus on. *Power* is the ability to express muscular strength quickly and efficiently, where *flexibility* is the ability to be mobile while being able to express strength through different ranges of motion.

If we intentionally develop a body around these four areas, then we are going to have a body that is durable, and resistant to injury and aging. During my time in the NHL, I actually got very attached to something called velocity-based training (VBT). What happens is you use a tool that attaches to the bar, dumbbell, or even your belt loop, and you can see how fast you are moving a certain weight so you have a constant feedback metric to understand if you are getting stronger week by week, workout by workout, because you are moving same weights at faster speeds.

You want to be able to test for each of these four areas so you can see where your focus may need to shift or where your priority for your training should go. Peloton classes may be great for a season, but there will be a time where you need to change the adaptation. Tests could be as simple as this:

- Muscular strength—three rep max for squat, bench, and a weighted rowing movement. Notice how you would test lower and upper body push and pull movements so that you are balanced.
- Muscular endurance—pushups in a minute and weighted wall sit for as long as you could.

- Power—long jump and seated medicine ball throw. Again notice the lower and upper body expression of power.
- Flexibility and mobility—seated toe touch reach. An easy assessment of flexibility.

Training and movement are a cheat code for longevity, healing, and true health. The thing is: it takes a life by design and knowing what is a priority to be consistent and get maximal benefits.

Incorporating Basic Habits

It is easy to get caught up in the fancy numbers and studies and come back to that state of confusion. This is why I want to bring it back to some very basic habits. Habits that you will begin to build over the course of a few months. You can begin to stack them on top of one another. You are likely already engaging in some of them. But what I wanted to be able to do was give you some big rocks to take action on that will have a big impact on your health and increase your ability to live differently.

For example, completing your workout earlier in the day not only increases the likelihood that you will get it done, but it also prevents your sympathetic nervous system from disrupting your ability to fall asleep at bed time and keep you out of deeper sleep stages. Taking a five-minute walk after every meal makes sure that your blood glucose levels stay more stable even due to the intake of food.

HRV (covered in detail in Chapter 4) is a great gauge when it comes to understanding how you are improving fitness levels because it is directly related to nervous system regulation and oxygen efficiency. Take note here, however. Since training is a stressor, as you are increasing intensity, volume, or frequency of training sessions, you may notice a drop in HRV for a short period of time. This is okay! It is the one foundation that when adding more to your life can cause a drop in HRV for a short period of time. A great question to ask yourself if you see a drop in HRV is: "Have I been engaging in more frequent, new, or more difficult workouts lately?" If the answer is "yes," it validates the awareness. As your body adapts and recovers, because you are focused on the other Pillars of Ownership, you will see an exponential rebound in HRV as your consistency increases.

If you are advanced in the domain of training and movement you are likely already engaging in some of the habits in this pillar. That is great! Now you can ask yourself where can you refine. Can you get some more advanced testing done? Can you begin to program your workouts a little more specifically so that you can see some different results?

A Simple Breakdown of Training and Movement Habits, Testing, and Tools

Life by Design Habits for training and movement include the following:

- Workout is completed up to two hours before sleep
- 30 minutes of intentional undistracted training per day
- 90 minutes of zone 2 conditioning a week (rucking, bike riding, jogging, stair climbing, rowing)
- Sprint 1× a week
- Strength train three days a week
- Get your heart rate above 80% for 20 minutes a week

- Move every 90 minutes (walk outside, yoga flow next to your desk)
- Walk for 5 minutes after every meal
- 10k+ steps per day

Enhanced personalized testing to further your ownership journey includes the following:

- VO_2 max testing (VO_2 Masters)
- Strength testing like grip strength and three rep max bench or squat
- Power test like long jump
- Muscular endurance test like max pushups in a minute
- Flexibility testing

Tools that could assist in the training and movement foundational principle include the following:

- At-home workout equipment
- Personal trainer (in person or app like future)
- Bar speed analyzer
- Heart rate monitors and wearables (see Chapter 4)
- Blood flow restriction cuffs

Foundational principle 4—Mindset

Mindset is where it all begins. For a long time I thought it was "woo hoo." I didn't fully buy into building it. As an athlete, I got my first mental coach at 13 years old. His name was Todd Herman (best-selling author of the book *The Alter Ego Effect*). We worked on a lot of things like meditation, visualization, and different stress coping mechanisms to keep me in a deep-focus state, or as we talked about in sports, "the zone." I thrived on it, but once I got into entrepreneurship and business, the practices I found so powerful lost their priority in my day.

I thought I could just push through with physical fitness and the mental toughness I had already developed would carry over into improving my capacity to handle stress. Well, I was wrong. Extremely wrong. And for a long time, it was my largest area of opportunity. There was a reason that I would easily get frustrated, overwhelmed, and anxious. There was a reason I often felt out of control and would forget things on a regular basis. When you try to control things out of your control, it is then that you begin to overthink. Overthinking leads to negative repeated thought loops, which in turn, leads to mental and emotional stress. That was a reason my mind felt like it was overflowing, and I would have stress reactions to the smallest issues that arose daily. I had not developed practices that built my mindset, and taught me to control what was in my control, the pillars and foundations. A mindset of inevitably amplifies that, but you have to do the work.

Mindset and mental toughness are associated but different. You can be mentally tough and still have poor mindset practices. This type of person has stress reactions to everything and simply pushes through. The consequence, however, is on your health and longevity. The body can't dissociate mental, emotional, physical, or spiritual stress, so if you do not have practices in place to help alleviate the mental, emotional, and spiritual stressors, they will continue to add more water to your cup.

Breathwork as a Mindset Practice

I remember the first time I did breathwork. I had an experience that allowed me to be connected to God in a way I had never been connected before. I felt a sense of calm and peace that was very difficult to describe. I felt whole for the first time. It had nothing to do with the breath itself, but involved areas internally I was able to heal and see clearly that prior were dark and murky. It made me feel different. It made me think differently. It caused me to want to explore it deeper as I was able to become aware of things I had not been before, such as:

- How my anger, frustration, quick temper, and stress responses were killing me from the inside out, while keeping me in chronic stress states.
- How they were disrupting my ability to take on more responsibilities, success, and develop deeper relationships because I lacked the ability to focus.

It set me on a path where I wanted more, but honestly didn't know where to start. With a kickstart from my wife, the mindset guru, I got my first coach as an adult, and there was an aha moment for how this work actually created the capacity to handle stress more effectively, change my reactions, and open a world that was not available to me before.

Two Important Questions about Mindset

I often get asked two questions that are so important in making sure the mindset controllable is touched on and looked after in a powerful way.

- What is the difference between *self-care* and *mindset?*
- Can my workouts, training, or physical activity be my mindset work?

The answer to the first question is simple. Self-care is something you do for only yourself (we hit on this in the Renew pillar in Chapter 8). It is not a discipline or practice that needs to be built. Self-care is something you should enjoy doing, it is energy-giving, whereas mindset work is exactly that . . . work. It requires energy and awareness. It is active, something that requires effort. You won't always want to do it, but it is that notion that creates growth. Mindset work is structured, on the calendar, and time is allotted for it so we can see growth and improvement. Things like journaling, breathwork, meditation, a coaching or therapist appointment all fall in that category. However, in self-care, we are just looking for renewed energy.

For the second question, the answer is 100% "no." Does that mean that during your training, yoga, or movement practice that you don't experience clarity or mindfulness moments? Of course not, but it will challenge you enough to create growth and really get deep enough to do the work to establish a change in your mindset and default reactions.

Mindset, Stress, and Chronic Illness

A Stanford University study proved shifting your mindset and being able to control reactions had significant positive effects on improving health, decreasing stress, and being able to handle life's challenges.[8] We actually do a stress reaction assessment at OWN IT to see what default stress reactions are in calm settings as well as what default stress reactions are during stress settings. It is called the ELI (Energy Leadership Index), made popular by Dr. Bruce Schneider. The ELI captures how you currently perceive and approach work and life stress. It measures beliefs, self-perceptions, emotional reaction tendencies, and behavior patterns. With the awareness and insights gained, you have the opportunity to reshape your attitudes and worldview to transform how you show up and handle stress.

Knowing that our body doesn't know the difference among mental, physical, spiritual, and emotional stress, being able to measure and bring awareness to your stress reactions creates a powerful tool at maximizing health. What we have found is that when you do the mental work and dig into the habits in the foundation of mindset, you see a significant increase in ELI scores. This has an exponential impact on how your body handles stress. Which is why this also correlates with the 40%+ increase in HRV.

Using HRV as an awareness tool to bring awareness to your mental state is powerful. When you have great training and eating habits, are in great shape, sleep well, but have a chronically low HRV, it is a signal that there is opportunity to mitigate mental and emotional stress by doing mindset work that can actually prevent the development of chronic illness. A growing area of research is the study of mindset on healing, but also the expedition of chronic illness. Patients who had done mindset work focused on love and gratitude created healing of illness, where stressed, angry, or poor mindsets actually caused illness and disease.[9]

Mindset, Anxiety, and Gratitude

The brain can't respond to stress and gratitude at the same time, which means it's one or the other. You can either experience anxiety, stress, and other negative states, or you can feel gratitude and all of the positive emotions that are associated with it.

You certainly do not choose to be anxious, but you can learn to control and choose your responses to what's happening. It comes back to controlling the controllables that interrupts the cycle of negative overthinking. When you focus on what you can control consistently and you take ownership over it, it is inevitable that you will get the desired outcome. You will have the patience that is required to forgo what you want now for what you want most. It will not happen overnight, but you can take a step in the right direction. With this mindset, if you were to improve your health by 1% every day for 365 days, by the end of the year you are going to be 38% healthier. Small and consistent efforts are what powers inevitability, no matter how big the changes seem. As you make small changes consistently, you will make the big changes seem small. It is inevitable.

Both anxiety and gratitude are perspectives on yourself, situations, and people in your life. Anxiety's outlook is negative, while gratitude's outlook is positive. Both have a degree of realism, but your brain doesn't know the difference between what is real or what is perceived. The goal in cultivating gratitude is to train your brain to hone in on the good and be mindfully present with it. When you practice gratitude, it prevents you from taking things for granted while keeping you present with what you are blessed with. The longer you do this, the weaker anxiety, fear, and worry become. Even better, you become increasingly more positive and appreciative of the good in your life.

Some of the habits you can develop like journaling, breathwork, meditation, reading, and prayer help increase awareness, but another habit is working with someone like a coach, therapist, or mentor. There is nothing like time collapsing the journey when you have someone who can call out certain areas and bring awareness forward to begin working on.

Making Mindset a Priority

The foundation of mindset is the place where you can make the most advancement, but is often last to be focused on and prioritized. Your mindset is one of your greatest tools, and leads to the inevitable outcome of either earning your health or your illness.

The world tells you to develop your mindset by never missing a day in the gym or constantly grinding away. Instead, you develop your mindset by doing hard things. Develop your mindset by not quitting. Develop your mindset by getting uncomfortable. Develop your mindset by keeping promises to yourself.

Life by design is about finding rhythm, and developing your mindset is about providing a moment of stillness to your day, drop the stress, regenerate, and empower your next intentional decision. That is why this foundational principle is so powerful. It single-handedly can create a change in your health. In all of the ownership moments you have been reading about throughout this book, each person has one thing in common: they became aware of how they were functioning and behaving and had a massive mindset shift.

The way you start does not have to be complicated as even 15 minutes a day can have a massive impact.

A Simple Breakdown of Mindset Habits, Testing, and Tools

Life by Design Habits for improving your mindset include the following:

- 15 minutes of meditation or breathwork per day
- 15 minutes of learning-based reading per day (Bible, books)
- 15 minutes of reflection or journaling per day
- 15 minutes of positive visualization per day
- 15 minutes of gratitude per day
- Mentorship connection 1× per week

Enhanced personalized testing to further your ownership journey and develop your mindset includes the following:

- ELI testing

Tools for building your mindset include the following:

- Meditation apps
- Breathwork apps
- Brain wave glasses

7

Pillar 3: Repair

"*We humans have lost the wisdom of genuinely resting and relaxing. We worry too much. We don't allow our bodies to heal, and we don't allow our minds and hearts to heal.*"
—Thich Nhat Hanh

IT IS NOT enough to build a house on a solid foundation, expose it to the elements, and never repair it. If you do, the neglected small repairs over time will become big costly repairs. Your body is the center of that metaphor. Repairing is a critical part of generating true health and optimizing your rhythm. It does not happen by accident, but rather by intentionally focusing on design. The foundations of sleep and immune response in this pillar are where you gain capacity and repair from the stress you have taken on. It empowers growth, and enables you to heal from the inside out. When you look at HRV (heart rate variability), the Repair pillar plays a crucial role that changes the entire game, and allows you to live life differently.

Foundational principle 5—Sleep

Sleep is like the Tesla super charger for your body, but yet we treat it like you are okay just plugging into a wall charger. For something that you should be spending a third of your life doing, there is such a lack of respect for it.

You are walking around chronically underslept, which leads to massive increases in internal stress that your body has to account for. When you sleep, the healing processes that occur are undeniable. It is when you are sleeping that the glymphatic system (the car wash for the brain) is 10 times more active, removing toxins from the previous day the brain had accumulated. It is when you are sleeping that the body repairs the muscles from tears due to working out, moving, and training. It is when you are sleeping that you transition into a parasympathetic or relaxed state and your entire system is able to down regulate and begin draining your cup from the previous day's stress accumulation. It is when you are sleeping that hormonal regulation is restored back to optimal levels, allowing serotonin and dopamine to be regulated, redeeming your mental and emotional states. That is just scratching the surface.

There is a reason that forms of torture include withholding sleep. In just one night of sleep loss, which is shown to be less than five hours, your reaction times, ability to modulate hunger, mental clarity, ability to regulate mood, and ability to handle stress all decrease. With two days of sleep deprivation, your human function more so resembles that of someone abusing alcohol or drugs. All you have to do is look at your HRV scores when you get poor sleep, or have poor sleep environments that impact sleep quality, to see how critical it is to managing your body's internal stress level and capacity. HRV scores can dip as much as 50% when sleep is poor. Sleep has continually been shown to be a habit that needs to be high on your priority list.

Two years ago, Tyler would have said sleep was the biggest challenge in his life. He was a new father, had an insurance business and a real estate brokerage that were both thriving, and to top it off, he was getting his pilot's license. His wife approached sleep as a non-negotiable and was very bold in making sure that she got the sleep she needed every night in order to function at the level she expected. Tyler, on the other hand, saw stealing sleep hours to work, send emails, and get more done as a badge of honor and something to be revered. He saw sleep time as wasted time, and continually stayed up late to ensure he was prepared for the next day.

He knew better, but the mindset behind it kept him in a downward spiral that stacked stress on top of stress, while at the same time shrinking his capacity to handle it. It was a double-edged sword that created a pattern where every two to three months he would break down, get terribly sick, and have to reset. He considered that pattern normal until the pattern was broken with a heart attack at age 43 and he decided he needed a change. I don't want your wake-up call to be a heart attack. Sleep is a foundation you cannot ignore.

Understanding the Circadian Rhythm

Your body has something called a circadian rhythm; you have likely heard about this before. It's a simple cycle between two hormones: cortisol and melatonin. Cortisol is high first thing in the morning and slowly drops during the day to an all-time low during your typical bedtime; while melatonin is high at bed time and slowly drops during the night to an all-time low during your typical wake time.[1] This cycle is what ensures you can fall asleep at night, and wake up refreshed and energized in the morning. What happens, however, is due to your lifestyle and habits, you get your rhythms turned around, and instead of going to bed tired and waking up wired, you go to bed wired and wake up tired.

Think about this for a second: cortisol release is your body's response to stress. Your bodies don't know the difference among mental, physical, spiritual, or emotional stress, as I have mentioned a few times. Thus, when you get exposed to stressors during the sacred evening hours, it impedes your ability to nurture the cycle and prepare your body for sleep, while leading your body to think you need to be awake because you are in danger.

There is a major difference between sleep quality and quantity. Quality being the amount of time spent in deep and REM sleep, while quantity being the amount of hours that you spent sleeping cycling among the four different stages:[2]

- Light sleep
- Slow wave sleep or deep sleep
- REM (rapid eye movement) sleep
- Wake cycle

The data shows that we want to aim for 50% of total sleep time in deep and REM sleep, which would constitute a high-quality sleep. Anything under 30% constitutes a poor-quality sleep, and no matter the length, even getting 8–10 hours at that quality will leave you waking up feeling tired and lethargic. It takes most people approximately 90 minutes to go through all four stages of sleep (plus or minus 15 minutes), and ideally, you are getting five full cycles of sleep each night, equating to the 7.5 hours of sleep you hear from the majority of the literature.[3]

When developing the habits for more high-quality sleep, the cortisol-melatonin cycle has to be taken into consideration. Designing your sleep habits around a consistent sleep and wake time is one of the most impactful and needle-moving habits you can implement to maximize sleep quality. The reason is, when you begin to go to bed and wake up at the same time, consistently within about 30 minutes, your body's release of cortisol and melatonin begins to become regulated. What happens in your body is that if you're typically in bed ready to sleep by 10 p.m. you begin to release melatonin at increased levels around 8 p.m., two hours prior to sleep time. When you stay up late working, are at a party, or simply ignore your bedtime, your body immediately goes into sympathetic, stress and protect mode. Your brain thinks, "Oh, my gosh, Justin is not sleeping, something is going on; he is in trouble; I need to increase cortisol and keep him alive." Even if you are just sitting on the couch or hanging around a fire, the response is the same. When you then try to go to sleep at 11 p.m. or midnight, your body is still in that stressed state and won't allow you to get into the deep healing and restorative stages of sleep (deep sleep and REM). Even if you sleep in, and get eight hours of sleep, the quality will have been severely diminished.

If you have ever woken up later than usual, felt groggy and not fully rested, this is why. Not only did you not get the quality of sleep you needed, but your body didn't release cortisol at the right time during the morning hours. This holds true with hitting "snooze." The reason hitting "snooze" is so hard on your body, and why you are better off getting up when it goes off the first time, is that a consistent wake time allows your body to release cortisol, which helps stimulate energy and alertness. If you hit the snooze button and allow yourself to start a new sleep cycle, the alarm 10 minutes later wakes you up before the new cycle is able to complete, disrupting the hormonal rhythm and causing more internal stress during a time when your body should actually be resting and recovering.

The 3-2-1-0 Rule

Sleep is so important, yet we take it for granted and fail to actually prepare for sleep. The 3-2-1-0 rule is an easy habit framework to use to help you prepare for the most important part of your day:

- 3 hours before bed: no major meals
- 2 hours before bed: no more work/stop heavy decision-making stress
- 1 hour before bed: no blue light
- 0 times: hitting the "snooze" button

Whenever you eat a major meal or take in food, not only does it increase blood sugar, but it also takes the blood from your brain and pulls it to your stomach to begin aiding in the digestion of whatever was eaten. Typically, during sleep, your digestive processes are slowed. When you eat within three hours of bed time, however, it puts you into a sympathetic and stress state, increasing cortisol and decreasing your quality of sleep again. You likely notice that when you eat close to bedtime, you will toss and turn through the night, wake up swollen, inflamed, and tired.[4] There is 400 times more melatonin produced by your gut than produced by the pineal gland in your brain,[5] so you can imagine how disruptive to the melatonin cortisol cycle eating late at night can be.

Two hours before bed, we want to stop making heavy decisions or working. I have so many people come up to me and say, my brain just doesn't shut off at night, and my response is, "yes, it does, you just have not allowed it the space to do so." If you are sending emails, text messages, planning for the next day, working with a vendor, trying to organize your calendar, in a fight with your spouse, debating where the kids should go to college or who is managing the play date tomorrow, right before bed, you can kiss goodbye your quality sleep as well. By continuing to stay active mentally and emotionally, you are raising cortisol, depleting melatonin, and putting yourself back in the sympathetic state. Having a boundary that starts two hours before your consistent bedtime allows your body to prepare and wind down for the most important thing you will do all day.

One hour before bed, you want to eliminate all blue light. This includes TV, phones, tablets, computers, and screens. Blue light plays an incredibly important role during the early morning and during the day to keep us alert and awake, but at night, for every 30 minutes of blue light exposure it suppresses melatonin release by up to one hour, again, disrupting sleep quality.[6] There are great filters you can put on your phones and computers. It is called night shift on the iPhone and you can set it so it pulls all blue light out before sunrise and after sunset. The same can be done on Android, and all laptops. For TVs, it is important to wear blue light blocking glasses if you choose to continue to be exposed to screens. At night, the amber, yellow, or red lenses are best as they take out 80%+ blue light versus only about 50% with the clear lenses.

Watching Your Caffeine and Alcohol Intake

Another boundary that is often missed is the use of caffeine. Which is why you should have a caffeine curfew, meaning you are no longer taking in any more caffeine. Caffeine has a half-life in the body anywhere from 6–10 hours.[7] Meaning, that if you took in 200 mg of caffeine at noon, somewhere between 6 p.m. and 10 p.m. there would still be 100 mg of caffeine active in your system. Then again, between midnight and 4 a.m., there would still be 50 mg of caffeine active. Only to have you take in another cup of coffee upon waking, adding another 200 mg to the 50 mg that was still left. Now why is this an issue?

There is a neurotransmitter in our brain called adenosine and its main function is to promote sleep and inhibit arousal.[8] However, to our brain, caffeine molecules and adenosine look the same.[9] So if we have caffeine chronically active in our system, it is going to constantly block adenosine from its binding sites, placing your body in a chronic state of stress. Your mind and body can never fully wind down, even though you may think you are able to sleep okay after ingesting caffeine.

I like to suggest a 9 a.m.–10 a.m. caffeine curfew. Yes, that is early, but when you begin to start aligning your habits, you will find you produce energy more naturally.

A substitute would be taking in a product that uses nitric oxide from beets to naturally increase oxygen flow in the body, which stimulates the same response as caffeine without the side effect of impacting sleep.

Alcohol is also a sleep killer. Recent studies have shown that alcohol is the number 1 inhibitor of quality sleep. Even one drink can have detrimental effects.[10] It decreases the amount of melatonin in the body,[11] increases snoring and sleep apnea, lowers blood oxygen levels, increases urination, and disrupts circadian rhythm—all which have a major impact in generating consistent sleep quality.

Developing a Menu of Habits That Work for You

I highly encourage you to create what I call a parasympathetic buffet. What this is, is a menu or list of things that make you feel relaxed and calm at night. What I suggest putting on here are all the things you enjoy and would want to participate in sleep preparation. Things like sauna, journaling, reading, walking the dog, stretching, watching a calming show, hot tub, meditating, warm shower, foam rolling, compression boots, or having a loving conversation. Those are all things that could be included, and by implementing the 3-2-1-0 rule at night, could begin to be added during the last hour before bed. When you have a pre-set list of options and a time slot that is held it eliminates decision fatigue, especially at the end of a long day.

When you are going to bed or waking up, another framework that can be implemented is the light, water, temperature, air framework.

At night, you would want dim, amber bottom-lit light to enhance a calming response from the body. You want to have a cool shower, or use something like the Eight Sleep to keep you cool by dropping your body temperature. You want to take in warm water like hot herbal tea to elicit a parasympathetic response from the body. Last, you want to add a breathwork sequence that is down-regulating. A box breathing exercise or any breathwork sequence that has a 1:2 ratio of inhale:exhale length (e.g., inhale for 2 exhale for 4).

In the morning, you would want bright, top-lit light (ideally the sunrise and getting outside; if not, a red light or artificial bright light is fine) to enhance the release of cortisol and other energy-producing hormones. You want to get exposed to heat like a sauna or set your Eight Sleep to get super-hot to wake you up, again eliciting a cortisol response providing energy. You want to take in 16 ounces of cool water with electrolytes like LMNT first thing in the morning to prime your cells and rehydrate them. Last, an up-regulating breath similar to a Wim Hof breath, two breaths in through the nose and one audible exhale through the mouth. Following this can not only keep your circadian rhythms in great sequence, but also really maximize your hormone and energy regulation.

The last habit to look at implementing good-quality sleep can be a little different. But, hasn't everything by now! It is called mouth taping. James Nestor, in his book *Breath*, does a great job highlighting the negative impacts of mouth breathing on your health. Mouth breathing impairs the amount of oxygen that you are able to absorb into the cells and use. Which is why if you snore or have sleep apnea you wake up with no energy. When you mouth tape, your body begins to establish the habit of breathing through your nose, but also increases your oxygen efficiency, oxygen absorption rate, and opens up the sinus cavity—not to mention the increase in quality sleep, reduction of respiration rate, and improvement in HRV and blood biomarkers.

Optimizing Sleep Even While Traveling

Travel is one of the most common disruptors of sleep quality, but it doesn't have to be that way. By making small and intentional decisions, you can actually begin to sleep just as well on the road as you do at home. A simple solution to be able to maximize sleep quality on the road is a travel framework.

When you are changing time zones, if you are there for less than 48 hours, stay on your native time zone. For example, when I go to Los Angeles from Miami for less than 48 hours, I will try to get to bed around 8 p.m. PST and then still wake up around 4 a.m. PST. It minimizes the shift needed and required. If you are there for longer than 48 hours, transition over to the new time zone using an app called Time Shifter. It helps you know when to eat, work out, supplement, and sleep by creating a plan for you two to three days before you leave, and how to adapt within a day of coming home. All you need to do is enter your flight information and a personalized plan is created for you.

Something we make for each of our clients is a sleep kit. These kits have a pillow case (the same one as they use at home), lavender spray, sleep mask, travel sleep hoody, recovery shoes, ear plugs, nasal strips, mouth tape, and curtain clips. This ensures that your sleep environment can be as close to your home environment as possible and mitigates the stress that otherwise would disrupt your sleep quality.

A few very practical tips when traveling to minimize the effect of time change is to not eat when you would typically be sleeping. If I use the same example as earlier, going from Miami to LA, I would not eat during the hours of 4 p.m. and 3 a.m. PST because that is when I would typically be sleeping. You see, sleep disruption while traveling often has a lot to do with how we are digesting food and processing our nourishment. This alleviates that.

Last, utilizing the framework of air-light-water-heat first thing in the morning can ensure you begin to adapt your circadian rhythm as quickly as possible. This means seeing the sun rise in the morning; drinking electrolyte-based water upon waking; getting exposed to heat through sauna, steam, or hot tub; and going through an up-regulating breathing sequence like Wim Hof breathwork. These small changes have such a large impact on ensuring your travel does not interrupt your quality-sleep habits, but solidifies them.

Tips for Tired New Parents

For new parents who do have to wake up in the middle of the night or who are struggling to get great sleep quality, try this napping trick. You want to keep naps to under 20 minutes or around 90 minutes to make sure you minimize grogginess, but to figure out the best time to nap, use this equation:

- Typical sleep and typical wake time (example 10 p.m. to 6 a.m.)
- Take the total sleep hours (example: 8 hours) and divide it by 2 (example: 4 hours)

- Add 4 hours to your typical sleep time (10 p.m. + 4 hours is 2 a.m.)
- Turn the a.m. time to p.m. by adding 12 hours because of our circadian clock (example 2 a.m. = 2 p.m.)
- Thus, 2 p.m. is the ideal time for a nap

This can be a way to get a few more quality-sleep hours in and chip away at any accumulated sleep debt from having disturbed sleep through the night.

Tracking Sleep Quality with HRV

When you look at HRV as a guide for sleep quality, it has incredibly impactful information. Look at the difference in HRV on a night where you drank alcohol and a night that you did not. There will be a significant difference. Try looking at a day where you did not use caffeine or had a curfew versus one that you did not. You will notice a major difference. Try implementing the 3-2-1-0 rule or the parasympathetic buffet versus just going to bed the same way you have always done it, with no intention, and see the difference. HRV is the guide to empower you to see inside your body and how your decisions are generating unknown stress, killing you from the inside out.

Sleep provides you with super powers and should be a key priority when trying to take ownership of your health and live differently. The world has trained you to believe sleep is the first thing that can be compromised in order to get more done, but the truth is the exact opposite. You want to feel, think, and look different? Then sleep has to be done differently, and this is where you start.

A Simple Breakdown of Sleep Habits, Testing, and Tools

Life by Design Habits for improving your sleep quality include the following:

- Consistent sleep and wake time
- 3 hours before bed no major meals
- 2 hours before bed no more work/stop heavy decision-making stress
- 1 hour before bed no blue light
- 0 times hitting the snooze button
- Seek light, heat, air, water first thing upon waking
- Set room environment to be dark, cold, quiet
- Mouth tape at night
- Create parasympathetic buffet

Enhanced personalized testing to further your ownership journey and improve your sleep quality includes the following:

- DNA testing (chronotyping, which helps you understand the natural circadian rhythm of how your body's clock gene is; in other words, whether you're a morning or night person)
- Hormone panel (to identify the cortisol cycle you're currently in throughout the day)

Tools for improving your sleep include the following:

- Eight Sleep (a sleep system)
- Mouth tape
- Travel kit
- DEP sleep shirt (a hoodie designed to help you sleep)

Foundational principle 6—Immune Response

I hate being sick. And I know so do you. It costs you more than just having to put up with the symptoms of whatever you are experiencing. It costs you time at work, time with your family, and disrupts the rhythm you have been able to establish in your life. What if I told you there were ways to not only increase your immune response, but decrease your sickness frequency exponentially? This is where HRV becomes such a powerful communication tool.

Your immune system has long been left to be developed by exposing it to illnesses to increase antibodies or to get vaccinations. However, through intentional habits and informed data like HRV, you can now be empowered to increase your immune system and know exactly how they are adapting to the stressors you are exposing them to daily.

Knowing When to Provide Extra Support

I want you to think of the inside of your body like a castle. All around the castle is a moat with a drawbridge and within the castle are millions of these little men and women warriors. What ends up happening as you incur stress in your life—mental, physical, spiritual, and emotional, real or perceived, positive or negative—these little men and women get pulled away to go and deal with that stressor. They have to decrease the inflammation, heal the area, and then come back to the castle. When you are under chronic stress, these little men and women are pulled away so often it leaves the castle understaffed. The viruses and bacteria that usually would be on the other side of the moat all of a sudden begin to pull the drawbridge down and start to storm the castle. That is when we usually get sick.

However, HRV will paint a picture as to how you are adapting to that stress and strain daily. When you see a three-day-in-a-row decrease of HRV or a single-day drop of more than 30%, it is a clear signal that there is something happening internally that needs to be supported. This is why you want to establish an immune protocol when you see either of those two things happen. That can be as simple as 3 doses of 300 mg of vitamin C per day until you see an increase in HRV, it can be 8 drops of oil of oregano until you see an increase in HRV, or it can be an immune supplement like Airborne. At OWN IT, we like to look at your cellular blood work and identify what is highly protective for you so we can build a custom immune supplement.

The trick here is that you only take the immune protocol until you see an increase in HRV, so that your body does not become reliant on what you are taking, but sees it as something to support it in a time of need.

The Benefits of Hot and Cold

We could not talk about immune response if we did not talk about hot and cold immersion through sauna and cold plunging. It has taken the world by storm, and we can all thank Wim Hof and social media for that one. Now, before we get carried away, I want to call out something very important. Both of these are stressors on the body. Are they positive stressors? Absolutely. Does science back up their healing properties? Without a doubt. What we must understand, however, is that HRV can help guide us on days that it may be more beneficial than others. Shocking that it is not always great to just push through doing something hard because someone said it was good for you. It may help, but maybe not today.

On an average week, you want to shoot for about 11 minutes total of cold exposure according to the Soeberg principle, but in order to determine which days you utilize cold immersion I want you to use HRV. On days that your HRV is above your 10-day average, it is an indication you are primed to take on more stress and have capacity to use the stressor beneficially. This ensures you are not stacking another stressor on a nervous system that is trying to adapt to what it is already overwhelmed by. The other myth I want to dispel here is that your cold plunge has to be 34°F in order to have an impact. It does not. The data shows that anything under 60°F is going to have beneficial effects.[12]

For the sauna shooting for 90+ minutes a week, broken into a minimum of three to four sessions is great, but it can easily be done every day.[13] If you have a traditional sauna, somewhere between 180°F and 220°F is a great place to start, but an infrared sauna will only get up to about 150°F. Both have their benefits, but you will just need extended time in the infrared sauna.[14]

If you have both implements at your disposal, a great way to go about this is to implement contrast therapy. What you would do is start with cold (1–3 minutes), then go into the sauna (15–20 minutes) and end with cold (1–3 minutes). Again, use the Soeberg principle as guidance. If you can't hit the total time durations, that is okay. Simply getting exposed to the hot and cold temperatures will have benefits. The easiest way to determine the temperature that is right for both the sauna and the cold plunge is, you want it to be uncomfortable but not painful, and work from there.

As I mentioned, the benefits of hot and cold exposure are immense. Studies have shown that repeated sauna exposure increases white blood cells and actually causes infected, dying, or diseased cells to die before they can infect other healthy cells, leading to increases in longevity and decreases in biological age.[15]

Data is also showing decreases in risk of dementia, depression, anxiety, and other mental health issues.[16] Similar to heat exposure, cold exposure shows a significant increase in white blood cells and T fighter cells signaling an increase in immune function.[17]

Not to be forgotten is that these are stressors and to be used in accordance to HRV, so long as to not continue to overflow the internal stress cup, but to be a habit and activity that helps it drain.

Red Light and Grounding

Another tool that is helpful when it comes to immune function is something called red light. Red light therapy uses low-power red light to activate the cell's energy generators or power plant, the mitochondria. Most of the energy made by the mitochondria is housed in a molecule called adenosine triphosphate (ATP), which helps your body store and use energy. Aging, illness, and lifestyle factors can make the mitochondria produce less ATP, which is why red light therapy triggers a reaction that helps reverse the decline and increase your body's immune healing powers. Using red light regularly as a tool has been shown to help repair tissue as well as relieve pain and inflammation.[18]

God has an incredible way of providing everything for us that is necessary for us to be in optimal health. Getting first sunlight exposure in the morning, last sunlight exposure at night can replace your red light, and getting your feet on the bare ground creates alkalinity in the body, the same impact as a PEMF mat (the acronym stands for "pulsed electromagnetic field"). If getting access to those two changes are difficult, that is where those tools have been shown to have incredible results for increasing immune function. The first and last light of the day is absent of the blue light, and enhances the movement of key immune cells (T cells), which increases their activation.[19]

When we get our feet on the ground, called grounding or earthing, it brings our body back to a state of alkalinity and reduces pain while altering the numbers of circulating neutrophils and lymphocytes. It also affects various circulating chemical factors related to inflammation, which basically means it decreases inflammation in the body, and we know what chronic inflammation leads to . . . chronic illness.[20,21]

With two young kids, Tyson was an entrepreneur who was constantly getting sick. No matter what he did, he found himself getting sick every two to three months, and would always be the first one to bring it into the home, which is obviously an issue with young kids. After trying every supplement, protocol, and medical suggestion, we, at OWN IT, had the opportunity to help him. After building a custom supplement for him based on cellular testing, getting him a morning and night routine with sauna and red light exposure, and establishing a personally designed framework for his HRV responses during highly stressful days, he doesn't even get sick during the cold and flu season. This is the power of a life by design.

A Simple Breakdown of Immune Response Habits, Testing, and Tools

Life by Design Habits to improve your immune response include the following:

- 100 minutes of hot exposure each week (sauna or steam)
- Cold exposure on days when HRV is above 10-day average (approximately 11 min per week)
- Immune protocol on three-day decrease in HRV
- 15 minutes direct sun exposure each day (preferably first sun/sunrise, last sun/sunset or combination of both)
- 20 minutes of direct contact with the ground each day
- Multivitamin every morning

Enhanced personalized testing to further your ownership journey for your immune system includes the following:

- Blood lipid testing (LPP)
- Cellular micronutrient deficiency testing
- Hormone panels

Tools for building your immune response include the following:

- Traditional sauna
- Infrared sauna
- Ice-up cold plunge
- Mito red light
- PEMF mat
- IV drips
- Ozone therapy
- Exosomes and stem cells

8

Pillar 4: Renew

"Almost everything will work again if you unplug it for a few minutes, including you."

—Anne Lamott

IT IS NOT enough to always be fueling, building, and repairing. You have to have space for fun, rest, and relaxation. Renew is the pillar of ownership you have likely forgotten. You believe it to be a waste of time or simply lack the awareness of what it includes. When you take a step back, however, and think about the last time you were cooped up in an office with no windows and only the sound of buzzing lights for weeks at a time, you quickly realize how important the two foundations of this pillar are to realizing true health. Self-care and environment play an integral role in minimizing stress and establishing a rhythm that can be seen in HRV (heart rate variability) and a life by design.

Foundational principle 7—Self Care

When it comes to the habit of self-care, the United States has done a great job at getting this wrong. Not only do you feel like you are not deserving of self-care, but it's been turned into a grocery list you feel like you have to do and no longer becomes de-stressing, but adds more stress. The definition of *self-care* is "something that you do for only yourself." It is not your meditation or breathwork. It is not walking your dog or coaching your child's soccer team. It is something you do only for you because it gives you joy, and is another hole in your cup that helps drain all different forms of stress.

There is a meme that shows a person giving one of his last puzzle pieces to another person, making them complete, and it said "the most selfless person." When I saw this, I immediately said to myself, "This is actually the most selfish person." The person giving the puzzle pieces is just like you. A leader. A parent. A business owner. A world changer. A mountain mover. You show up for everyone but yourself, and you give pieces of yourself away to complete others, but there will come a time when you don't have anything left for someone who really needs it. You won't have any puzzle pieces for your wife or husband. You won't have any puzzle pieces for your kids. You won't even have any puzzle pieces for your mission. You will have burnt out, and it will have not only cost you your health, but possibly your life. When you say "yes" to everything, your "yes" begins to mean less. Boundaries and standards elevate our ability to act on our best "yes."

The most selfless person is the person who ends up empty and depleted at the end of the day, but is willing to set boundaries and provide self-care for themselves, so that they can fill back up and go do it all again the next day. Those boundaries and self-care activities are completely individual, and different for every person. The only similarity is it is something that is solely for you.

A Story of Self-Care

I had a call with one of my clients very early in the start of my career. He was a three-time *New York Times* best-selling author and had a book due in six weeks. He had five chapters to write and he had hit a wall. No creativity, no focus, no clarity, no desire to write. He had been on the go a lot with five kids and a beautiful wife, but he was beginning to panic.

On our call, I asked him, "When is the last time you did something for just yourself?"

He laughed and said, "Justin, I have five kids on summer vacation, a wife who wants to spend time with me, and a book deadline in six weeks that I have not written. When am I supposed to do something for me?"

I changed the question: "If you did do something for yourself, what would that be? What do you love to do?"

He responded. "I love to water ski. I have not been in almost two years, though."

You have to understand that this man lived on a lake, with a boat, and a kid who loved to drive the boat. I said, "For the next three weeks, I want you to take one hour three times a week and go water skiing." After some initial resistance, he reluctantly accepted.

After the first four skis, he texted me agitated saying, "Nothing is happening." But I urged him to stay consistent and keep going.

On the fifth session, it was a Thursday, he called me around 1 p.m. I could hear a lightness in his voice, a joy. He said loudly over some wind, "Justin, we are still on the boat. We have been out here for almost four hours. I had a breakthrough while I was skiing this morning. I wrote the whole thing in my head. I have clarity and a knowing I have not had in a long time. I am free." He was not broken. He just had no puzzle pieces left. He needed some self-care time to give him the capacity back to have a creative mind, and think clearly.

You are the exact same. Your cup is full and needs to be drained.

Establishing and Tracking Your Self-Care Routine

Establishing a rhythm is not just something that is optional, but something that is required in order to find true health. It has been shown to exponentially increase the benefits of stress resilience and capacity.[1] Americans cited benefits of self-care as enhanced self-confidence (64%), and increased productivity (67%) and joy (71%). From a physical health perspective, self-care also reduces heart disease, stroke, and cancer.[2]

This is why the habit of self-care is very simple: you just need to build out 30 minutes of self-care a day. This can be broken down however you like. Two sets of 15-minute intervals. Three sets of 10-minute intervals, or simply getting it all done in a 30-minute block. This will have significant and exponential results in improving capacity and realizing true health if you are willing to do this consistently.

In terms of what the activities should be? That is 100% up to you. Remember the definition of *self-care*: "something you only do for yourself." That is why I suggest making a self-care buffet, similar to what you did for the parasympathetic buffet sleep habits in Chapter 7. When you have a list of 5–10 things that you know you can pull from on any given day, it eliminates a decision you have to make. Decision fatigue is real, and if you have to make a decision about how you will pour back into ourselves, the likelihood is you just won't do it.[3]

It could be as simple as having a massage booked on repeat every two weeks, and then knowing on Tuesday and Thursday you go to the sauna. It could be watching a mindless TV show because it is something that completely relaxes you. I have seen many people begin to stack cellular healing practices in their self-care routine, sitting in the hyperbaric oxygen chamber or lying in front of the red light bed while reading their favorite book. Any of these things are acceptable and makes it simple and efficient to be able to find time for you. The other days simply pull from your buffet, but the time is already held on your calendar.

When looking at self-care, HRV is again a powerful awareness tool because even when everything else is in alignment and you see a dip in HRV, it is a sign you have not poured back enough into yourself. HRV can become the trigger, and if you are willing to take ownership, you will be empowered to make a quick change. It is not weak to pour back into yourself, but a sign of strength. A foundational principle in a life by design.

A Simple Breakdown of Self-Care Habits and Tools

Life by Design Habits for adding self-care to your rhythm include the following:

- 30 minutes of self-care per day
- Build a self-care buffet (something just for you) with ideas like these:
  - 10-minute breathwork
  - 10-minute meditation
  - 10-minute quiet walk outside

o Book a weekly self-care treatment (massage, spa moment)
o 10-minute quiet reading
o 10-minute red light

Tools you can use for self-care include the following:

- Red light
- Hyperbaric oxygen chamber
- Compression boots
- Vibration massage tools

Foundational principle 8—Environment

We had just moved into our new apartment in Miami. On the list of life events when it comes to ranking stress, moving is top three, right up there with death of a family member and loss of a job. So as you can imagine, when I walked into the apartment that I was seeing for the first time, and it was half the size I thought it was, it did not go over too well.

Immediately, I began to feel claustrophobic, and it felt like the world around me began to cave in. Panic filled my chest and my breathing became shallow. I began to sweat and could feel my heart beating out of my chest. "I can't stay here," I said aloud. "I can't stay here, I have to go to a hotel."

As my wife rolled her eyes and came up to me slowly, she wrapped her arms around me and said, "It's okay, I will make it an environment you can thrive in, it's only temporary." As she wrapped her arms around me, I instantly began to feel better. My heart rate dropped, the anxiety drifted, and my breathing slowed. The hug that I originally wanted to shake off, I suddenly didn't want to end, and 10 seconds later, I felt my body melt.

I tell you this story because I think you underestimate how important your environment is. It is everywhere, and is the guide that shapes human behavior. The environments you are in either level you up and enhance behaviors or they slowly tear you down and degrade your health and consistency. You have likely become so numb to the environments you live in daily that you find yourself operating in a major environmental default. You have become a thermometer instead of a thermostat, adapting to whatever is around you instead of dictating the environment.

Your environment is all around you. It is your bedroom, your office, your car, your home, the music you listen to, the podcasts you engage in, the people you hang around, the way you travel, the city you live in, the family outings you participate in. Every single thing you do has an environment and it has a drastic impact on your health. It is one of the hardest foundations to pinpoint what is influencing HRV, but it is also one of the biggest influencers because of how many factors are involved.

A Story of Environmental Factors

Try taking a look at your HRV when you travel versus when you are at home as a teaching tool. The stress of traveling and the outside environment will have a negative effect on HRV, which is why it is so critical to have a framework to travel locally or internationally.

Ava is the CEO of a business that operates out of Japan and has to make trips every two months for a week. It had taken a toll on her and she was on the brink of quitting a job that she loved because of what it had done to her health. She had gained 30 pounds; it would take her multiple weeks to catch up from the time zone changes leaving her exhausted, and she had begun to notice episodes of mental breakdown. It was crushing her because she loved her job and the position, but did not see a way out.

After a workshop I did for her company, she came up and began to ask me questions. On the spot, we began to build her a travel framework that included how to adjust to time zones within 24 hours, a personalized supplementation routine during the flight, food timing, and built out a sleep kit full of products for her to make the journey much easier on her body. A month later, I saw her at another workshop for her company, and she came and gave me a huge hug as tears welled up in her eyes. She was not the same person. She had more energy, her smile was bigger, and I could tell she had lost some weight. All she said to me was, "Thank you. What you did changed my life."

I want you to realize, I did not do anything other than help her build a life by design.

The Power of Connection

Environment even includes the people you are around and your interactions. This is why if you get in a fight with your spouse and spend the day in constant tension, you will see a drop in HRV the next day. Or on the opposite side of the spectrum with a single hug, you are able to decrease stress levels and increase oxytocin and dopamine, the happy hormone, within your body.[4]

It was actually found that you need four hugs a day for survival, eight hugs a day for maintenance, and 12 hugs a day for growth when it comes to your health and how you feel love. Try going without any positive physical contact for a few days and see what happens to your HRV. It is a stress factor that will be added to the total score, and can cause it to drop. Remember, your body keeps the score.[5]

Alyse and I have a habit that we have instituted that we both initiate two 10-second hugs a day, so that we can ensure each of us is getting the connection that we need, regardless of how the rest of the day is going. But it is just not physical contact that needs to be a habit. We take for granted the environments we are in every day and the small changes that can be made to make sure we set our environments up well. Exchanging candy jars for fruit bowls, or steak sandwich lunch stations to salad bars at the office. These environmental changes help shape your habits and determine which ones will be the most consistent.

Changing Your Physical Environment

Have you ever been working in an office next to a construction yard where there is constant beeping and crashing? The first few days it's annoying, but then after a few days it begins to dissipate. It becomes white noise, but you have to realize that your body is still having to cope with the stress it is providing. You might have noticed that as time went on you began to be more irritable, easily frustrated, tired, and even possibly got sick during that month. That is the subconscious environmental stress, or noise pollution. Even though you don't "hear" the construction anymore because you have gotten used to it, it doesn't mean that your body isn't having to deal with the internal stress it is developing. This can happen with music, podcasts, doorbells, shared workspace, dogs barking, or anything else for that matter, which is why designing your environments is so critical.

Alyse turned the space in Miami into a home, and the office into a positive environment. In our bedroom, she put up blackout curtains so the lights of the city didn't keep us from deep states of sleep. She put Eight Sleep on our bed so that we could individually sleep as cool as we needed, and get woken up with heat and vibration instead of an alarm. She put lavender spray on both her and my pillows so that it had a calming sensory stimulus every time we walked into the room. She made sure our Sonos speakers system was connected throughout the house, but that our bedroom was on a different channel so that we could play calming meditation or binaural beats to fall asleep. In the office, she put my red lights up on the wall so I could turn them on first thing in the morning, when I begin working before the sun is up. She put the yoga mat next to my desk so that I could easily do five minutes of movement every couple hours without having to think about it and make a space. She made sure the desk was positioned so that there was plenty of natural sunlight.

On top of all of this, she built me a sleep kit for traveling that had the same pillow case we sleep on at home, the same lavender spray, the same candle, curtain clips, blue light glasses, and blue light blocking stickers for those pesky LED lights in hotel rooms. No matter where I was in the world, my brain would think I was at home and minimize the stress on the nervous system.

As I talk about these environmental factors, I hope your brain is turning. We spend 100% of our days in one environment or another. If you add up the time spent in your home, your office, and your car, it probably equates to 90%+ so those are likely the highest priority environments to check on light exposure, temperature, smells, and ease of access to sunshine.

It does not have to be complicated to begin to stack environmental habits along with the other pillars in Chapters 5, 6, and 7. For example, moving every 90 to 120 minutes, from the foundational principle of training and movement, could go easily with getting outside for those movement breaks to change up your environment. The 3-2-1 rule for the foundation of sleep can be incorporated into your sleep environment. Watching the sun set at night can be a part of your self-care or mindset foundation.

Thinking about the Intangibles

Environment is all around you. It's not just the physical things, but the nontangible things. You can all remember a time where you listened to a podcast, watched something on social media, or began to listen to music that drastically changed your mood and what you were thinking about. Those things are all a part of your environment and all things you have control over.

I do a YouTube show called "Championship Mornings" with the main purpose being to expose people to the concept of environment and that nobody's morning habits are the same. Something that has stood out, however, is how uniquely people have curated their environments. For me, my morning consists of getting exposed to bright light. I wake up with the sun on my deck every morning because it resets my circadian rhythm, but it also is where I do my breathwork peacefully. I wake up with my Eight Sleep at 110°F so I wake up hot only to step out into the Florida heat, which again wakes me up and increases cortisol first thing in the morning. I have my water bottle sitting on the counter with my custom OWN IT supplement and LMNT already waiting so I can prime my cells for absorbing water the rest of the day. The space is curated, all by design.

It is no longer acceptable to just exist in your environment because you are now aware that your environment is everywhere. By simply existing and being the thermometer, you are living by default, which will get you results that are good enough, average, and mediocre. Instead, take ownership of your environment. If you can't control certain things within the environment, control what you can. Dictate how long you stay in a certain place, or how long you engage. Put up boundaries that will allow you to be the best version of you while you are in those environments.

I think a lot when I am traveling. I have a Delta Lounge pass by design. The craziness of the airport creates compounding stress, and with the amount I travel, it is important that I can have a place that is calm and restful. During holidays with my family or spending time with the in-laws, Alyse and I still set boundaries. We still go on date night so that we get our alone time and are able to connect.

There is power in your environment. What I want to empower you with is the awareness that it is everywhere, and that by setting certain parameters, you can own every environment you are in and generate a life by design.

A Simple Breakdown of Environment Habits and Tools

Life by Design Habits for improving your environment include the following:

- Watch sunset at night
- Wake up with the sun in the morning
- Morning routine (light, heat, air, water)
- Sleep environment (dark, cold, quiet, smell)
- Aware of working and living environment (temperature, noise, social interaction)
- Connect with someone you have a deep relationship with daily
- Five 10-second hugs a day

Tools for improving your environment include the following:

- Red light
- Hyperbaric oxygen chamber
- Compression boots
- Vibration massage tools
- Aroma therapy
- Sleep kit
- Standing or sitting desk
- Quality chair in office

PART

III

Live Different

9

Creating a Life by Design

"A man who stands for nothing will fall for anything."
—Malcolm X

IT'S ONE THING to see everything laid out nicely with the four pillars and the eight foundations of ownership, but it's a whole other thing to be able to turn that into a life by design and understand how to organize it and start. Remember one of my promises at the beginning of the book was that you would learn how to build a life by design, not just provide a list of options. That's what you'll dive into in this chapter.

The definition of *design* is "a plan, system, and process created for a specific purpose." Remember, you don't rise to the level of your goals, but rather you fall to the level of your systems. What the world has done is put you in a process without a specific purpose, without something built for you, which leaves you wondering why you don't get where you want to go. You are in a life of default, and now we're about to change that. It's time for your design.

First Things First: A Focus on Preparation

A positive consequence of a life by design is optimization; however, *optimization* used to be thought of as being over the top, and required perfection with massive restriction, when it actually has nothing to do with perfection but rather the pursuit of better. It is, in fact, the only place health can be found. You need to know what your body needs, not what everyone else tells you that you need. There is freedom in this because you can control the controllables and forget the rest. Focus solely on what you have to prepare.

I want you to see preparing as a way to empower and lead yourself to beginning a life by design, but realizing your ability to live life differently will be directly correlated to your ability to prepare. Here's what you need to do:

- Purposeful Priorities
- Replace
- Expend
- Patient Practice
- Accept Accountability
- Rest, Reassess, and Refine
- Expect

Purposeful Priorities

You cannot do everything at once. If you tried, you would be disappointed with the results. The Pareto Principle says that

80% of outcomes come from 20% of inputs, meaning if you prioritize the foundations of ownership that are your weakest, it will help build your foundation on rock. When you prioritize something, it becomes a guide to how you make decisions, which will allow you to ask better questions like: what do I need? Who do I need? What testing should I get done? So that your efforts are fruitful and focused.

This is why tying HRV (see Chapter 4 for more on heart rate variability) to your habits and behaviors is so critical. You will become empowered to understand what habits need to be the highest priority for *you*, not for anyone else, or anyone else's agenda.

Replace

Notice how I say *replace*, not *add*. I see it all the time: you are made to feel you need to continually add new habits to your routines because your best friend, coworker, or favorite influencer on Instagram told you it worked for them. You end up with a laundry list of habits that actually pulls you away from what works for you. I don't care how perfect you think you are. You will always be required to replace certain habits and behaviors. I put all of my habits and behaviors under fire each quarter, to see what needs to be replaced or what can stay.

What will serve and prepare you in one season will not serve and prepare you in another, and honestly, it can hold you back. You will have to replace behaviors. There are habits that may have served you, shaped you, prepared you for where you are now, but will not get you to the next level of where you need to go.

Expend

Life by design will require you to expend energy, time, or resources. Health is not passive. It cannot be set to autopilot. That is how you fall back into default. That is how you got here. A life by design is *active*. So many business owners automate, delegate, and outsource to find success in business but you cannot do that in your health and establishing a life by design. Nobody is coming to save you, and nobody will do it for you. You are the knight in shining armor you have been waiting for. Once you expend, the return on investment from a focus, energy, productivity, and quality of life standpoint is exponential.

Patient Practice

You will not get a life by design right on the first try. There will be bumps in the road, you will get thrown off; the transformation may even be slow, but persistence and patience make the outcome inevitable. When you begin a new life by design you can get thrown off because of life events or entering into an unfamiliar season. You can feel like a beginner, and start to believe you are not good enough or it isn't working. That is okay, but you need to be patient. You can't cut corners and expedite the work; it takes time. Consistency over intensity. When you are patient and show up consistently, it only becomes a matter of time before the result is reached.

It's easier to go from failure to success than from excuse to success because you are moving forward. The best excuse is the worst excuse because it becomes a lie that will control the rest of your life leading to earning your disease. It is not perfect practice, but patient practice that becomes a lifestyle.

Accept Accountability

Dissociating yourself from the outcome and focusing on the process is what is required for a life by design. You may have put a sleep improvement metric or an energy increase expectation as your sign of winning, but I need you to change your thinking. Accepting where you are, accepting accountability for being there, and focusing on the process is what is required to make this a lifestyle. No matter how long your road ahead or how much improvement your health requires, accepting accountability puts you in a position to prepare in a way that is different and ensures the outcome you desire is inevitable. You cannot simply pay the fee to change your health; it requires you to take ownership and be accountable. There is going to be an outcome either way; it might as well be the one you want, and the way to ensure that is by accepting accountability.

Rest, Reassess, and Refine

The world tells you if you are not moving or rushing around, you are doing it wrong. You need to rest and recover in order to grow from the stress you are exposed to, and reassess how your life by design is working for you. A life by design has iterations. This is not a "set it and forget it" type of thing. It takes refining, and no habit may be right for you forever. Seasons change; you change, and just as your life is constantly being refined, so does your preparation. When seasons change, so do your priorities, and when your priorities change, so do your systems, and thus, your design needs to shift to stay in alignment. Refining is what keeps you out of default.

Every quarter, Alyse and I take a weekend just to ourselves. No phones, no business, no family, just us. We connect and give ourselves time to just be together, but in the afternoon on the first day, we pull out our calendars to look at our design over the last three months. We assess our wake-up times, our morning routines, night routines, self-care time, training routines, date nights, working and living environments. We even get our blood drawn during that meeting so that our team can reformulate our nutrition and supplementation routine. This is the reason for our expedited progress in all things health and life: a life by design. Rest is a weapon, boredom is a killer, and wisdom can discern the difference.

Expect

You have prepared. You have been consistent. You have ownership. Now expect a life that reflects that! It never ceases to amaze me how many people prepare for something and then are surprised when it happens. The redemption of your energy, focus, sleep, or whatever it is for you is ready for you as long as you are ready to prepare for it. Consistency with preparation leads to inevitability. That is the exciting part. The results you get are simply the lagging effect of your habits. You are going to get a result whether you like it or not, so why not design it around the one you want? It's yours, now take it.

Asking a Few Important Questions

I want you to get really good at asking better questions of yourself so that you can determine your own personal journey for realizing true health transformation and bring awareness to some key points. There are certain questions I want you to ponder and carry around so when you find yourself struggling to establish certain habits, or see downward trends in HRV you can begin to come back to them. Everything here is extremely powerful and important, but if we don't get this alignment right, it won't matter.

I want you to invest a few minutes on each question in the following sections so that you can draw a line in the sand as to what you will or will not stand for. You are more than able to generate a life by design, but are you willing? Getting clarity here will empower you to take ownership of what you are about to design and where you start.

What Are Your Top Three Core Values in Health?

You may have done this for your business, you may even have done this for your family or yourself, but very seldom have you ever thought of these in the context of your health. When you think about core values, they are personal ethics or ideals that guide you when making decisions, establishing habits, and solving problems. Identifying the values that are meaningful to you can help you develop a life by design that you can take ownership of and execute consistently.

As an example my three core values in health are:

- *Flexibility*—I travel a lot so every habit I develop needs to be flexible in order to maximize consistency. That is what creates sustainability.
- *Accountability*—I need to establish a team around me to hold me accountable. I have a couple different workout partners, I have a mental performance coach

I see regularly, and I use HRV every day to help guide
me and keep me honest.

- *Excellence*—I know that everything I do is a reflection
  of how I show up, and my health is the ultimate dem-
  onstration of that. If I am not in excellent health it is
  because I do not have excellent habits, and thus, cannot impact in an excellent way.

As you get clear on what your core values are when it
comes to your health, you are better able to establish a sense
of consistency when it comes to the behaviors you are need-
ing to change and habits you are looking to establish. As
you begin to live differently and see the impact on your
HRV, it will only strengthen the value and create a deeper
rooted instinct within.

I have listed a few words here to get your mind going, but
you do not need to choose any of them. You can choose your
own, or maybe they are even values that you have established for yourself personally. Either way, I want you to write
down your three to four core values that you can own in
regards to your health.

Accountability	Achievement	Adventure
Authenticity	Authority	Autonomy
Balance	Boldness	Challenge
Community	Competency	Courage
Curiosity	Cutting Edge	Dedication
Determination	Excellence	Flexibility
Fun	Growth	Happiness
Honesty	Humor	Influence
Inner Harmony	Intention	Knowledge
Leadership	Learning	Love

Ownership	Peace	Performance
Pleasure	Poise	Recognition
Reputation	Respect	Responsibility
Results	Security	Self-Respect
Simple	Stability	Success
Whole	Wisdom	

When you have your values in the domain of health, I want you to ask yourself the following question: are my current habits and behaviors aligned with my values when it comes to my health?

What Does Your Priority Tree Consist Of?

This question you need to continually come back to. There is a reason why preparation starts with priority, and it is here that I want you to identify yours. You want to get your health under control, but you can't do it all at once.

If your health is a priority, then you will be willing to make the steps accordingly. I always say, show me your calendar and I'll tell you your priorities. If you are wanting to change your environment and get around more friends to increase your social health, but you don't have time scheduled for it, then it is not a priority. If you are wanting to lose weight or get stronger and you don't have your workouts scheduled, then it is not a priority. If you are wanting to get better quality sleep, but you don't have a nightly wind down system scheduled, or a set bedtime reminder, then it is not a priority. You schedule every other meeting for your job, business, or kids' social events, but have failed to do that for yourself. You will constantly find yourself in the same position, and as we have learned, you are simply earning your illness, not your health.

When you build your priority tree, try to organize it as a set of five. You can use my name coding or you can use your own, but since health is holistic, and incorporates all of life (mental, physical, spiritual, and emotional aspects), we have to prioritize in order for it all to work and be sustainable. My five priorities are:

1. Faith—This is my foundation and key to my spiritual health.
2. Self—If I don't look after myself and pour into my own health holistically, I can't serve or look after anyone else at the capacity needed.
3. Spouse—My most meaningful relationship.
4. Friends and family—A major part of my mental and emotional health.
5. Business—My passion and what I love.

If it makes the tree, it is important. When I say *priority*, I am not meaning *time*. Even though my business is fifth on my priority list, I absolutely spend the most time on it, but when I am doing my monthly priority audit, I am putting my highest priority on the calendar first. For example, nothing will take the place of Sunday church at Vous. No business meeting, no workout. Nothing will take the place of my sauna and breathwork for 20 minutes midday. No meeting. No business lunch. Nothing will take the place of date night. No holiday. No work opportunity.

Once I have the highest priority habits on the calendar, there is always more than enough room for about 14 hours of work each day. But more importantly, the work time is fueled, energized, and inspired. That is how you start to create a life by design.

I want you to create your priority tree. On the left side, put the current order, and on the right side, what you desire it to be.

Questions to ask yourself each month:

1. What does my priority tree consist of and what do my current behaviors tell me about my priorities?
2. What is the foundational principle that needs to be prioritized?

What Are You Optimizing for, and What Is on the Other Side of This Journey That Isn't Available to You Now?

This is one of the greatest testing questions to ensure you have focus and consistency on your health journey. Seasons in your life will change, desires you have will shift, and priorities will adjust. If you are not clear on what you are optimizing for, your health will constantly be elusive. You will be taking actions, but unfortunately you will be living in fake health, and quite possibly, without even knowing it. Consistency is the multiplication factor on this journey that will make it sustainable for the first time in your life, and help you earn your health rather than your illness.

Ask yourself:

1. Where in my health am I wanting to see change, and are my current habits going to get me to where I want to be?
2. What foundational principle has the habits that will help me optimize that area?

What Does Your Accountability Team Look Like?

This is the question that keeps you honest. You can pretend to take ownership of a life by design, but the outcomes will speak for themselves. This is why an accountability coach or community creates exponential increases in results. A coach can provide frameworks that you may otherwise take years to figure out. Like helping you set up a framework for your assistant when booking travel so they know what your nonnegotiables are. They might be that your hotel has a gym, a sauna, or a grocery store within walking distance so you can maintain your consistency on the road. It might be building out a sleep kit for travel so anywhere you go you have access to a sleep mask, earplugs, lavender spray, curtain clips, and a sleep supplement so you are prepared for anything that is out of your control.

At minimum, your accountability team should be something measuring HRV to continue to generate awareness for you. It is a metric that doesn't lie. It has no emotion or bias. It simply communicates with you how your body is adapting to the stress and strain you are placing on yourself due to your habits, behaviors, and lifestyle choices. It prevents slipping back into default by maximizing your awareness, but you have to be willing to bring the context. If you are noticing you are not getting to where you need to go, do not settle. Do not believe the lie that a life by design is impossible and not meant for you. Sit with this . . . if you could do it yourself, you would be there already. It's time to ask yourself a better question.

Ask yourself:

1. How am I measuring the impact of my current habits?
2. Do I have the appropriate accountability team to get me where I need to go?

Taking Small but Specific Action Steps

With the clarity of values, priorities, and needs you now have, I want you to get specific on action steps. As with anything, not everything is great for you, nor is it always good timing; so starting small and selecting one pillar or two foundations to focus on is where I want you to begin. The pillar and foundations I want you to focus on are the ones you feel need the most improvement, or are currently the greatest area of opportunity. They likely resonated heavily with you as you were reading Chapters 5–8. To establish your actions, I want you to go through the framework in the following table:

Life by Design 1
Pillar
Foundation
Habit
What value drives the implementation of this habit?
What will you gain?
What is currently in your way?
What is the first step to implementation?

An example would be like this:

Life by Design 1	
Pillar	Repair
Foundation	Sleep
Habit	3 hours before bed: no major meals
What value drives the implementation of this habit?	Excellence because I know I sleep poorly and my HRV drops as much as 27% when I eat late at night, impacting my mood, mental clarity, and energy, which does not allow me to show up in excellence.

Life by Design 1	
What will you gain?	Daily energy and mental clarity, while also having more creativity to continue to grow and impact the way I want to. It will also help with weight loss and fight against dementia, which my family has a history of.
What is currently in your way?	I work too late, and by the time we are done cooking dinner, sometimes it's closer to 8 p.m.
What is the first step to implementation?	My assistant will set 6:00 p.m.–6:30 p.m. each day as my wrap-up time so I can complete working every day by 6:30 p.m. I will set relaxing music to come on throughout the house at 6:30 p.m. as my trigger. Each Sunday, at 1 p.m. on the car ride home from church, Alyse and I will have a conversation so we know the cooking schedule for the week. She cooks three nights a week and I cook three nights a week.

This is what design looks like. Specificity is key. You need to set a specific time and place so you can establish the boundary and visualize yourself in the location. When you get specific you can also establish a timeline, which makes identifying the impact on HRV even more impactful. Again eliminating your need to have to make decisions.

Each morning you can arise and look at your HRV and ask yourself the question to increase your ability to understand your body: how is my adherence impacting my HRV?

The Phases of Forming a Habit

The world tells you that in only 21 days you can develop a new habit. It seems good, short enough to be motivating, but long enough to be believable. Unfortunately, that is not true and there is no data to support it. In a study conducted at the University of London, researchers found the actual time it took to build a new habit was, on average, 66 days. With the variance being anywhere from 18 to 254 depending on the circumstance, complexity, and environment. However, what held constant was that behavior change and developing sustainable habits was based more on a system of consistency and accountability rather than goals and perfection.[1,2]

So as you begin to develop your life by design, I want you to realize there will be four phases you need to progress through to live in full ownership, and you will be able to identify them by how you are feeling. They are:

1. Plan
2. Routine
3. Rhythm
4. Instinct

Plan and Routine

As you get to this stage of the book, you likely know what pillar, foundation, and habit you are going to prioritize and have a plan for tracking with HRV. You have also begun to hold times on your calendar and design your days, and very quickly stepped into the routine phase.

But here is the thing: a routine is an event. It relies on a person, place, or thing. It either occurred or it didn't. It usually has to happen at a set time, or a set place, and travel, delays, holidays, or unforeseen circumstances disrupt it.

A habit, on the other hand, is a process and has a system behind it. Which is only reached through consistency. Knowing consistency needs to be a big part of the system, it becomes pretty apparent why people struggle because, in the past, it took so long to validate behaviors. Donald Edmondson, Ph.D., principal investigator of the Resource and Coordinating Center for the NIH Science of Behavior Change (SOBC) program says, "Behavior change is hard. Yet sustaining healthy behaviors is one of the most important things people can do to live long healthy lives."[3] It can be so hard to appreciate the impact of habits on a day-to-day basis because you don't see their impact until many months or even years later.

> You can get to sleep on time a few nights a week, but you are still tired.
>
> You choose the salad and protein for lunch, but you still have weight to lose.
>
> You go to the gym for a week, but you're still out of shape.
>
> You meditate first thing in the morning, but your anxiety is still sky high.

This is why the use of HRV is so powerful. It is called proactive "experimental medicine."[4] It provides immediate insight as to how the behavior is impacting your rhythm, increasing your awareness of its impact, thus increasing consistency. This is why I call it accountable consistency. When

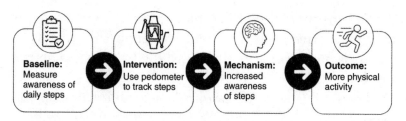

Figure 9.1   Creating new habits.
© John Wiley & Sons, Inc.

you have someone or something holding you accountable, there is no sliding by the truth, which will expeditiously slide you into the critical phase three.

Figure 9.1 shows how we will be using HRV and empowering you with the personalized guidelines as to how to slowly create new behaviors and habits that mean something for you!

Rhythm and Instinct

As you begin to see the impact of HRV on behaviors, it increases your consistency and thus has become connected to the process and not the outcome. This allows you to get into a rhythm that you can begin to love and feels like you no longer have to think about it or force it.

The more consistent your rhythm becomes, the faster you shift into instinct. This is where the habit you have been seeking to develop becomes automatic and a part of who you are. You no longer have to work out at 6 a.m. in order to get your workout in. If you had an early flight, you simply shift your day around and prioritize it for when you land or later in the evening, but it still gets done because it is an instinctual part of what you do. The outcome is inevitable when you have built a system that works for you. It is no longer a routine. It's a life by design. There is freedom here.

There are 3 laws you can implement that will help you expedite the journey from Routine to Rhythm and make it feel more attainable.

1. **The Never 2 Law**—This law states that you will never miss two days in a row of a new habit you are trying to develop. Meaning if you miss Monday you won't miss Tuesday, if you miss Saturday you won't miss Sunday. Even if you did this for an entire month you would end up successful 16 of 30 days, which is consistent. It gives you a place to start and build.

2. **The 30 in 30 Law**—This law states that for 30 days you will find 30 minutes a day to devote to that new habit. Whether it is planning, scheduling or executing.

3. **The MVP Law**—This law states that there is a Minimum Viable Progress (MVP) for any given day when something in your day blows up. Meaning if you can't get your 30 minute run in, get 5 minutes in because that is what is what you can do today. The act of still getting your shoes on, and getting outside not only continues to build the habit, but the likelihood you will do more than you thought increases significantly.

The following tables provide tangible examples of what happens when you add these three laws and accountability to your plan and routine in order to reach rhythm and instinct.

When You Stop at Plan and Routine

Habit	Plan	Routine	Rhythm	Instinct
Cooking dinners at home	Get all the groceries on Sunday and set a time to cook for yourself	Every day at 6 p.m., you begin cooking what you bought	You get bored, thus it interrupts the transition to rhythm, so you need to find a new plan	NA
Breathwork at lunch time	Set an alarm to go outside at noon and do breathwork	Every day at noon, you sit outside as your alarm sounds	You hit "snooze" on the alarm so it interrupts the transition to rhythm, so you need to find a new plan	NA
Stretching before bed	Put a stretch band and mat next to your bed	30 minutes before bed, you stretch	You stay up watching Netflix and this interrupts the transition to rhythm, so you need to find a new plan	NA

When You Stop at Plan and Routine

Habit	Plan	Routine	Rhythm	Instinct
Drinking ½ your body weight in ounces of water	You buy a water bottle and put it at your desk	You make sure you drink three bottles of water a day	You forget the water bottle as you walk around throughout your day, so you need to find a new plan	NA

When You Add in the 3 Laws and Accountability to Reach Rhythm and Instinct

Cooking dinners at home	Get all the groceries on Sunday and set a time to cook for yourself	Every day at 6 p.m., you begin cooking what you bought while you call a friend or family member	No matter where you are, you are calling a friend or family member reminding you it's time to cook	You don't have a family member call, but you are up cooking anyways
Breathwork at lunch time	Set an alarm to go outside at noon and do breathwork	Every day at noon, you sit outside as your alarm sounds and meet a friend	Even if you are not together, you do the same breathwork at the same time	You do breathwork anytime throughout the day on your own

When You Add in the 3 Laws and Accountability to Reach Rhythm and Instinct

Stretching before bed	Put a stretch band and mat next to your bed	30 minutes before bed, you stretch while you brush your teeth	No matter where you are, as soon as you begin brushing your teeth you start stretching	You travel to another city and you stretch without even thinking while brushing your teeth
Drinking ½ your body weight in ounces of water	You buy a water bottle and put it at your desk	You make sure you drink three bottles of water a day and send a checkmark to a friend at the end of every bottle	As you travel or get busy in your days, you still send the checkmark	Drinking less than three bottles of water a day, you now feel extremely dehydrated

An Example of Developing Instinct

There was a message from a client I saw a few months ago. She had long been a stop-and-go gym goer and never someone who was able to stick with it consistently. Due to the fact that she hated it, she never made it a habit and never saw results. She struggled with her energy and weight, but really wanted to make a change. Over the course of four months, she built a system that was sustainable for her and had us as her accountability team. One morning, she was talking to someone at the gym as she was leaving, and as they parted ways, the person said, "Have a great day; see you tomorrow."

It was the "see you tomorrow" part that hit her so hard. The only reason she would see her tomorrow was because they would see each other at the gym. She had become a regular. It was at that moment she became aware she had established a new instinct. A new habit that she had ownership of. A life that had a different design than before. A year in, and she doesn't even remember what it is like not to be a gym goer as it is a regular part of her life. She travels regularly and it becomes a part of her day no matter where in the world she is. Life is different.

Testing and Tracking the Habits That Are Right for You

Here is the cool thing about using HRV on this journey: it doesn't only empower you by understanding which new behaviors are most impactful for you, but it can also be a wake-up call to a habit that is hurting you that you were unaware of. You can put the behavior up against what we call the "HRV test" and see what your body is communicating. For example:

- Have a couple glasses of wine before bed, and watch your HRV drop in the morning.
- Have coffee late in the afternoon to get a burst of energy instead of getting outside or doing breathwork, and watch your HRV drop in the morning.
- Work out late at night versus early in the morning, and see what happens to your HRV.

Allow your body to be the guide—not the study you weren't involved in, or advice from an expert who doesn't know you or have context into your life. Empower yourself and be your own study.

That is the beautiful thing about what you are learning here: this process can now help you decide what is meaningful for you and what is not, when you should do something versus when you should not. This framework gives you the flexibility to not live in perfection and a deep set of rules, but rather to live in fluidity and have a way to measure the impact of your choices.

Breaking through When You're Struggling to Implement a Habit

Sometimes there is a habit that you are wanting to develop that you know improves your HRV, feels good, and is critical in getting you to where you want to go, but it has just felt difficult to get to the rhythm and instinct stage. I have experienced this many times in my life, and in the life of my clients. Even a habit that is instinctual can get thrown off during a season of large life change or drastic shifts in priorities. For example, you move across the country and your workout habit gets totally thrown off, or you welcome a new baby to the family and your night routine gets blown up. These things will happen, but what should you do? There are a few things you can do immediately:

- Go back to your preparation questions (which I list earlier in this chapter) as they will help realign your priorities and establish an understanding of where to start.

- Establish an accountability team. This could be hiring a coach or expert who can help guide your journey or engage in a community of like-minded people who are trying to accomplish a life by design like you are. When you are held accountable by people outside of just yourself, it increases success rates exponentially. They keep your path narrow so that you can learn, grow, and see the results you are searching for in less time.

- Try to habit stack. The idea behind habit stacking is to attach your desired habit to something that you already do instinctually, while at the same time maximizing efficiency. For example, if you wanted to focus on the foundation of self-care and the habit of adding 15 minutes of breathwork and stretching to your day, you might try to simply place a block on the calendar. Instead of just adding the 15-minute block, what you might do is strategically add the block right after you take your dog for a walk since that is something that you already do instinctively. This increases your consistency and immediately increases your chances for success.

  Or if sleep was one of the foundations and the habit you wanted to add was not eating three hours before bed, instead of just trying to use will power, a first step could be brushing your teeth after your family dinner so there is less of a desire to eat after brushing your teeth. The family dinner is something you already do consistently, so ending your meal brushing your teeth is a way to increase speed of adoption to the new habit.

Here are some additional examples of habit stacking.

Desired Habit	Current Instinct	Habit Stack
100 minutes of sauna a week	Meditate for 20 minutes a day	Do your meditation in the sauna
3 hours before bed: no more food	Brush your teeth at night	Brush your teeth right after dinner
Zone 2 conditioning 3 days a week	Workout 5 days a week	Use zone 2 conditioning for 20 minutes as a warm-up before your workout 3 days a week

The beautiful thing about building a life by design is that nothing is set in stone. You are in control because you are controlling the controllables and building a strong foundation based on what you need. The more you understand your body, the stronger your foundation can become. It doesn't matter how old you are, or when you start, you have the same right to your health and the changes that come with consistency. When you live a life by design you are able to identify your formula to win. Not just once but repeatedly. A system that allows you to live differently than everyone else and get results that are not available to everyone else, thus making you different. When you live differently, life looks different. You have the ability, but are you willing?

10

Taking Ownership

"Responsibility equals accountability equals ownership. And a sense of ownership is the most powerful weapon a team or organization can have."

—Pat Summitt

I OPENED UP my left eye, and then my right eye. I removed the tape from my mouth that forced me to breathe through my nose all night and jumped out of bed. I walked out the patio door to snap a photo of the sunrise, only to lead into my five minutes of breathwork, Bible reading, and prayer. Energy was oozing out of my body. As I walked inside, there was a knock at the door, and I let the phlebotomist in to take my quarterly cellular blood sample, which would turn into my new supplement formulation for the next quarter. Within 15 minutes, I was downstairs in the gym, with my workout plan and water in hand, and with mental clarity, excitement, energy, and drive that I had been chasing for a long time in my life. When you live a life by design, everything you have been chasing suddenly turns around and begins chasing you.

Finally, I had found it. A life by design that resulted in experiencing true health—a life that is truly different from the rest of the world, with a rhythm and set of habits that works for me. The gratitude that fills my heart knowing this is my reality is beyond words, and can only be demonstrated by living differently forever and never going back.

This is available for you too, but it requires a wake-up call and paradigm shift. You have to be willing. You have to want it. You have to do things differently. You have to want the energy, vitality, focus, and mental clarity that is waiting for you. I hope this book does that for you. I hope it shows you what is possible. I hope it shows you how simple it can be. I hope it shows you how different you can be. I hope it causes you to see what you considered normal before may actually be hurting you. But reading this, understanding it, and doing nothing does not get you there. I need you to act on it.

As you develop your life by design, choosing to never go back to "normal" will be your commitment to consistency. That is what will make your success inevitable. What you know now cannot be unseen, and thus, you will only want to live differently.

It will be different than what you are used to and require parts of your life to look different, but you are in the process of breaking the pursuit of normal, and your future self will thank you for it.

When you adopt an ownership mentality, you no longer live for perfection but rather for consistency. Author and pastor John Maxwell told me years ago, "Long-term consistency beats short-term intensity every single time," meaning your consistency in a life by design over perfection is a part of the winning system. As my dad said, "Talent gets you noticed, but consistency gets you paid," and this sentiment continues to ring true.

I want nothing more than for you to be successful. It lights me on fire when I hear of someone realizing a breakthrough by living differently. I want you to experience that as well, and when you do, please message me and tell me your story. It is by the testimonies of others that you show others it is possible. If you are struggling or are in need of a coach or community in order to be consistent and overcome obstacles, please also contact me. That is why OWN IT exists: to support people just like you and see you through to a different way of living. I have made available many free resources to aid in your journey at www.thepowerofownershipbook.com You will find videos, frameworks, pdf and printable guides to help you take ownership and live a life by design. You have the roadmap and community in front of you. You are no longer alone. You are no longer hopeless. You are no longer confused on where to go. You have clarity, confidence, and you make the choice.

Everyone can start, but champions finish. They don't finish because they're more talented than you. They don't finish because they grind harder than you. They finish because they know the outcome is inevitable and simply are consistent longer. They out-wait everyone else with patient endurance knowing they are controlling what is in their control, and have built a system that cannot lose.

You are a champion. It's inevitable that you will have abundant energy. It's inevitable that you will sleep deeply.

It's inevitable that you will lose weight. It's inevitable you will have focus and clarity. It's inevitable that you will feel well. It's inevitable that you will earn your health. Knowing the truth, that you are playing your game and nobody else's, will give you the patience required to be consistent long enough to realize those results.

You will redeem your health because you got consistent. You are more than capable, and it's already prepared for you. It is time to prepare yourself. Your new tomorrow starts today.

Welcome to The Power of Ownership; life is different here.

11

Ownership Moments: You Can Do It Too

"And they overcame. . . by the word of their testimony."
—Revelation 12:11, King James Version

I WANTED TO provide you with encouragement and testimonies so that you can see yourself in someone else. By the word of your testimony, others can overcome it as well. You can redeem your health and live life by design just like any of these people. Normal will always be after you, but will never overcome different.

32-Year-Old Entrepreneur

As a young girl, I experienced physical abuse and homelessness. These traumas cultivated a fear for survival. Desiring a more stable life, I committed to chasing high achievement. This thirst ultimately led to Harvard, and subsequently, building and selling multiple successful companies. But that's not where I stopped. Fear had been driving me and I knew no other life. I went on to study quantum physics and teach subjects from blockchain technology to block universe theory.

And while I received many accolades and built a heroic resume, ultimately the biggest challenge I faced in my adult life was realizing that I was nonetheless depressed, addicted to drugs, and living a lifestyle that was quickly killing me.

My health was of no consequence to me. In trying to prove my worth to the world, my well-being suffered. I eventually found myself completely burnt out, not just mentally and emotionally, but physically where I couldn't even get out of bed.

Therapist after therapist, doctor after doctor, I could not find the answer. I shifted my focus to finding help elsewhere. I wish I could say I found OWN IT, but in divine timing, OWN IT found me. I was able to quit Adderall, alcohol, and nicotine. Through accountability, I was able to address my reactions to daily stressors and [OWN IT] helped me learn how to use my internal energy more effectively. I began to meditate, which transformed my inner world. Today, a daily, two-hour meditation practice sits as the foundation for connection with myself and my spirit.

Before I would wear sleep deficit as a badge of honor, but as I became introduced to HRV and was able to understand my sleep data, it empowered me to see sleep as a foundational pillar to my well-being; I went from sleeping an average of four hours a night to nine hours a night. Over my life by design journey, my resting heart rate went from an average of 86 to 42, and my heart rate variability went from an average of 14 to 111.

It wasn't until OWN IT that I learned that physical well-being cannot be separated from spiritual growth and conscious evolution. In fact, becoming whole is the only way to find true health. OWN IT did for me what doctors and hospitals could never do. Today, thanks in part to OWN IT, I'm not just surviving, I'm thriving.

43-Year-Old Entrepreneur (Company Exit at 39)

As a young man who prided myself on my entrepreneurial endeavors, I was used to pushing and striving with no awareness as to the impact on my overall health. As I led my team through a sale and exit during Covid, I suddenly found myself in an emphasized realization of a similar feeling most would call burnout. This was far from what I had felt previously, however. I was burnt out physically, mentally, and spiritually. All my prior best practices around holistic health had fallen to the wayside. My biggest symptoms were low energy, high fatigue, and generally low or confusing motivation (the post-exit world of a founder feels a lot like an existential crisis with a lack of grounding and lack of meaning). To add to that, we were going through a lot of life transition stuff (new homes and travel), and there wasn't a lot of stability, structure, or routines in our life.

I started with OWN IT with the intention to get back to a solid baseline of physical health without knowing how much of a Band-Aid® approach that really was. As I began to learn about HRV and different foundations that made up health in a holistic way, it provided a framework and structure that, for the first time in my life, made sense. Something that would allow me to build systems around that could hold me accountable and empower ownership of my own health for the first time. A life by design.

Today, I have been able to establish frameworks that work for me, and are flexible based on the season and priorities in my life. The systems, although they have shifted and adjusted, are still inspired by my original starting point, while being held together by my understanding of HRV. It inspired a number of things that went into my current routines, habits, and life structure (especially around nutrition, movement, hydration, self-care, and mindset). Realizing that health was holistic and that our bodies did not know the difference among mental, physical, spiritual, and emotional stress was a paradigm shifter for me that has become an integral part of my everyday awareness, thanks to the ELI. In fact, it was the catalyst to my path to choose coaching as my new vocation.

49-Year-Old Executive

Before taking ownership of my health in December 2020, I was beginning to put the pieces in place to build momentum. I had just purchased a new property for our business, my daughter was getting married, we were renovating our home, and it was the height of Covid, and I knew health would be a massive factor for me. My initial thought was I needed to get a workout plan in place to make sure I was fit and strong, as that is what I thought health was made up of. Boy, was I wrong.

As soon as I was introduced to HRV and the concept of the four pillars of ownership, it shook me to the core based on my baseline numbers. I had an HRV average of 20 and often found my sleeping less than five hours. Then it happened in January; I got Covid and will never forget the wake-up call it gave me, and that I needed to look at my health more intently. My brain fog was more than I usually suffered from, my energy level kept me effective for a half day at best, and I knew I could not continue at this pace. I knew I needed more health in a holistic fashion.

Diving deep into the four pillars, I had never known a lot of what made so much sense. I actually needed a holistic overhaul, not just a new workout plan. And I can honestly say I am playing at a level I have never been at before. My mental clarity, focus, energy, and zeal for life is not like anything I could have imagined possible. It is a completely different normal. In fact, it is not normal at all. The power of emotional healing, mindfulness, and awareness as to what it would take to be a leader has elevated every aspect of my health. Taking my HRV average all the way to 67.

While the personalized frameworks have helped me bring more intention to my routine, I now get my "A" game every day, and ownership has empowered me to do this. I have been awakened to the power of holistic and integrated health in a way that only makes sense. You cannot segregate or piecemeal here; it takes a lot of intentionality and a solid daily system for it to work. Today, I wake up energized and cannot wait to start the day, bringing my best to both my family and business. My family and employees see a different person who is much more aware of the environment, acts with intentionality, and cares deeply for each individual. Ownership has been the key for me. . . . It starts here and ends here. . . . I have never wanted it more. It is the best way to live.

43-Year-Old Entrepreneur and Founder of a Recruiting Brokerage

It's true what they say about being an entrepreneur . . . it's a roller coaster. One day you're riding high on how amazingly well your business is doing and the next day you're ready to throw in the towel.

The lifestyle becomes a mantra, until it doesn't and you realize something needs to radically change. This was exactly how I lived my life. Everything revolved around my business. It defined me and who I was (insert big red flag here). Although I loved what I did, had passion around my business, and thrived on the success, there was something that started to take a major toll . . . my health and well-being.

I was stressed the majority of the time. I wasn't getting quality sleep. I didn't have time to do things that I enjoyed because there was always another meeting, another phone call, another proposal that I needed to tend to. I couldn't be present with my family because my mind was focused on my business. I ignored it for a long time. My friends and family always told me how inspirational I was and had the perfect life being a wife, a mom, a sister, a friend, a daughter, a strong business woman. From the outside, I was living a dream life.

I would hear that and think this is how it's supposed to be. This exhausted and ill feeling is what it required. I'm looked up to, admired, I'm an inspiration. I told myself I didn't need to change a thing. When the stress and anxiety started to become overwhelming, I knew I needed to make a change before it was too late. If I valued my life, my family, my everything, I needed to start focusing on my mental, emotional, and physical state.

Through understanding what ownership was all about, my eyes opened to how I was serving everyone and everything around me with great discipline. The one person I wasn't serving was myself. I made excuses, pushed off things that I enjoyed doing. Me time and doing what made me light up was almost nonexistent.

I'm a "tell-me-the-facts" kind of person and learning what my body was telling me through HRV and other bio-markers was very persuasive. I instantly knew I was earning my illness and not my health. Immediately I began to live differently and change the habits and behaviors based upon the four pillars of ownership.

I took time to do the things I already knew I loved to do. I also started going deeper and finding out what else lights me up and incorporating more of those things into my life. I was alive again and it felt exceptional!

I won't lie and tell you it all came super easy for my type-A, control-everything personality. It was a challenge that I found myself trying to fight against at times. I kept at it and stayed consistent. This time for myself.

The result has made me a better version of myself, for myself. A better partner to my husband. A better mom to my children. A better person to be around.

Do I slip back into my old ways at times? Sure I do. The difference is that now I have the systems, team, and under-standing how to bring myself back to the more vibrant and alive version of me that I learned still existed from discover-ing OWN IT. And for that, I'm forever grateful!

47-Year-Old Real Estate CEO

Despite my regular CrossFit sessions and strenuous work-outs, my health was in dire straits. My challenging lifestyle, dietary missteps, and persistent stress had paved the way to obesity, pre-metabolic syndrome, fatty liver disease, sleep apnea, nocturnal hypoxemia, and low testosterone. In short, I was on the precipice of type 2 diabetes, a compromised quality of life, and a potentially early departure.

Just when I was grappling with the fear of my health's inevitable decline, I was introduced to the concept of a life by design and OWN IT. Despite having collaborated with elite coaches in various aspects of my life, I had never encountered someone who shared my vision for longevity and reversing aging.

The diagnostic approach to understanding my health gave me a structured plan to counter my health concerns and enhance my performance. Utilizing heart rate variability (HRV) as a guide for health management, I was able to gain insight into my training, nutrition, and lifestyle behaviors, and for the first time, I had a tangible metric to direct my health journey.

Our first step was DNA assessment, unveiling inflammation triggers such as caffeine, salt, and lactose, and a genetic mutation in the MTHFR gene. We addressed my chronic dehydration, setting water intake targets that noticeably improved my hydration and reduced headache frequency.

I was given a curated meal and supplement plan designed around my lifestyle—a regimen that was not just palatable, but enjoyable. Together, we revamped my training routine, making it manageable and tailored to my preferred activities.

By examining intracellular nutrient absorption, we identified deficiencies in B6, B12, oleic acid, and CoQ10. My gut biome evaluation revealed mild inflammation and dysbiosis. Adjustments to my supplement intake and timing, along with a custom vitamin blend, helped address these issues.

We also designed strategies for optimal performance during travel, social events, and challenging holiday seasons, incorporating a weekly diagnostic performance review.

The transformation has been remarkable. In just one year, I have lost 23 pounds of fat, reduced my body fat by 7%, added 6 pounds of skeletal muscle and 3 pounds of lean water weight. My resting heart rate now places me in the athletic category, with my heart rate variability improved by 24%. Furthermore, my liver enzyme levels and blood markers have normalized, where type 2 diabetes is a fear of the past.

In essence, I have fully redeemed my health. My performance is at an all-time high, improving across all metrics. I am experiencing a harmony among my mind, body, and spirit I never thought possible, with my vision of a vibrant, energetic, and fulfilling life within reach, I find myself a better father, husband, and business leader. The positive impact I am making in the world is a testament to what a life by design can do.

43-Year-Old Entrepreneur

Health, to me, has always been around metrics. As a lifelong cyclist, I thought health was about body weight, power, heart rate, and watts. This way of living differently opened my eyes and mind to the fact that health is more holistic than just numbers. Utilizing tools such as breathing and meditation, mindset transformation, and hot and cold therapy are additive to the health journey.

Being in a state of ownership means that you don't only work on what is seen on the outside, but rather you start with what is happening internally. Begin with the mind and body, and then utilizing state of the art technology, provides an optimal blend and metrics to allow the ability to stay on track.

Endurance athletes struggle with looking "healthy," but middle age means loss of hormones and muscle mass. My "normal" was a "skinny" 150–155-pound cyclist. I found myself constantly tired between all my rides and running my business that I began to see a major drop in the way I was leading and performing.

By utilizing HRV, genetics, and the system that a life by design had provided through personalized habit formation, I was able to add 20 pounds of muscle mass and a transformative amount of energy. Now I can maintain single-digit body fat at a truly healthy 175 pounds. I'm strong, my wife thinks I look good naked (!) and I have the energy to work all day as an entrepreneur and still have the energy to travel and chase around my 11- and 13-year-old boys.

Right before I found OWN IT, I faced a turning point in my life; my mother had died, and I was in a major season of growth and scale in my business. I knew it would take all the mental focus and power that I had. My life up to that point had solely revolved around grinding to performance, and I knew I needed to shift toward holistic health but did not know how. Being the best leader, husband, and father that I could be is no longer a dream, but a reality because I have a winning system that is built for me. What is amazing is that OWN IT distills complex information and concepts down into a personalized guide—a roadmap to build the optimal version of yourself!

Just as important, I worked through this process with my wife. We not only focused on the external factors and metrics that could improve each of us individually, but we also learned about what we could do internally, spiritually, and as a couple. This top-down approach has been absolutely amazing and truly life-changing. It's one thing to look and feel good physically. But knowing that you are living your best life with your partner is truly amazing!

We can all get in the car and pull out a map and find where we would like to go. But which road do we take? With Google and Apple Maps, Waze, etc., we are confident in the path we are taking. It also changes in real time, based on what is going on at that moment. What if you could have something like that for your health? This process not only gives you your map, but it also gives you the system for real-time feedback, coaching, and even the supplements to make it as easy as pulling up Google Maps on your phone. With this type of technology, I just can't ever see myself going back to the "normal" way of regular medicine—where you wait to get sick before taking action. Now I feel like I own my health.

54-Year-Old CEO Corporate Executive

I like to think of myself as a forward-thinking leader who empowers his team well but often forgot about myself in the process. What I did not realize was how much more was available that I was completely unaware of.

I was finding that the team was running out of energy, the typical "zing" that was so well received in the office was gone, and people were getting sick more and more. I was getting sick more and more.

It began to not only overwhelm me, but also create anxiety that I had never had before to a point where it was making me chronically ill. When I stepped back and looked at what I was doing day to day it was hard to realize how out of touch I had actually gotten and how much of a life by default I was actually operating in. I was staying up late to send emails and eating even later just to keep my alertness. I had gained about 50 pounds in two years and could feel my health slipping away.

I had been at a leadership conference and that was the first time I heard Justin speak. Immediately everything made sense and it was a wake-up call I needed. Before I had never known the solution, only the problem, and did not have the capacity to figure it out for me or my team. I immediately brought him in and he changed the way I and the rest of my team live. We now live a life by design. We block mandatory time for lunch to allow a change in environment, we over-hauled the snack room, and even put in a little recovery center right in the office.

Not only has the "zing" come back to the office, but the sickness rates of everyone have dropped, the insurance claims have dropped, and the productivity of the team is better than ever. Without becoming aware of these items in my life, establishing a life by design system, having a system to be accountable, my life and business would look very different today.

49-Year-Old COO Executive Leader

As an executive who has spent his entire life striving for more, I had finally hit a wall where more was hard to come by. I had gained weight, had no energy, and my ability to focus was shot. I no longer wanted to travel, and knowing that I was underperforming because of my health was causing me a lot of anxiety. I went to the doctor to see what was going on and I came away with four medications because I had pre-diabetic levels of blood sugar, high cholesterol, and hypertension.

I had just lost a family member to a heart attack and I knew I could not get into this pattern of living the same way and trying to medicate my way out of it, so I chose to do something different. It was then that I found OWN IT and began to live a life by design. I developed a travel framework so I did not suffer from jet lag anymore, and could keep my nutrition and training in check when I was on the road, along with having a personalized solution for my sleep, supplementation, and stress management practices. The best part was that I did not have to figure it out myself. I was able to be the student and simply execute.

Today, I feel like I have ownership over my health. I have dropped 75 pounds, I am no longer pre-diabetic or suffer from high blood pressure, I am on no medications, and I don't remember ever having this level of energy. I feel like I am leading better than I have in my entire career and that life is just beginning.

40-Year-Old Hedge Fund Manager

For the last 20 years, I have been working my way through a career in finance in New York City. The lifestyle was always normal to me: late-night dinners that included a couple drinks every night. Getting up early to get a workout or run in, having two to three coffees while looking at the markets, and not eating for most of the day.

Last year, I began to notice anxiety that I had never had before and my energy levels were making it hard for me to keep up, even though I could not get in much better shape. I ran the New York City Marathon and finished in the top 100, so physical fitness has always been a priority, but I could feel I was not healthy.

I heard Justin's philosophy through social media and I wanted to explore more. I got a wearable and was shocked when my HRV was consistently 13. I did not know why and I needed help. Immediately we began changing the way I lived. I began waking up in the morning, and instead of going right for coffee, I started with water, electrolytes, and breathwork in the sun. I designed my day around lunch meetings instead of dinner meetings, while also cutting my alcohol intake down about 85%. The personalized approach to how I designed my life was what made these changes sustainable and impactful for me.

Now my HRV is 51 and I have more energy than I have had in years. The anxiety I was feeling is now nonexistent, and I did not realize how poorly I was sleeping until I actually got a good sleep.

There should be no other decision other than to live a life by design because it has changed my life and I will never go back.

You Are Not Broken

I hear it all the time, "My genetics are against me and that's why I'm overweight, can't sleep, work all the time, and have high blood pressure." "I have a deviated septum and that's why I can't breathe through my nose which is why I can't run or sleep, causing me to gain weight." Rather than taking a look at the dysfunctional habits and behaviors that have become normal, take a stand and say "Enough is enough."

Understand it has nothing to do with your genetics, but everything to do with the environment you create and the habits you embody. Be willing to take ownership of the fact you don't work out consistently not because you have kids but because you don't make time. You don't get to bed at a regular time, not because you are too busy but because you have not instituted boundaries and non-negotiables at night. You can't breathe through your nose not due to a deviated septum, but because you don't engage in habits like daily steams, mouth taping, aroma therapy, low-intensity nasal breathing, or daily breathwork. You have thrown in the towel and accepted the outcomes. You are expecting a change without making a change, expecting a different outcome without doing something different. You are giving away your power, accepting mediocrity, and then believing that there is something wrong with you or you are innately broken.

Let these words be empowering: There's nothing wrong with you. You are not broken. You are perfect just the way you are, but you are too great to stay the same. You need to stand up and say, "I am going to be different. I am going to behave, act, and choose to be different. I am not going to pass on ownership, but rather empower myself on the path to redemption of my health. I am done with being passive and conforming. That stops now." These people who have shared their stories in this chapter are just like you, and may they be inspiration to you, exposing you to what is possible.

We had a client come to us who could not figure out why her health was deteriorating: her weight was increasing, she could not sleep, her blood pressure was high, she was pre-diabetic, and suffered from high levels of fatigue and lethargy. She came to us saying, "What is wrong with me? What is not working properly?"

We have to change the narrative. The question is not "What is not working properly?" The question is "What am I doing daily that is not allowing my body to work properly?"

She was on insulin and high blood pressure medication, using caffeine to stay energized, but none of the doctor pre-scribed interventions were changing anything . . . because she wasn't broken! Nothing was internally wrong; instead, how she was living was causing the breakdown! She was so unaware of how she was living and had no idea the impact. She traveled across the country at least twice a month and did not have a framework for how she adapted to the time zone change, so the travel disrupted sleep patterns every two weeks. She was on a plane traveling at least five other times a month, eating whatever was convenient. Her on-the-go snacks from the airport were full of highly processed sugar, seed oils, and artificial sweeteners. Her morning exer-cise routine consisted of a 45-minute walk. She worked 15+ hours a day, 6 days a week, and regularly found herself eat-ing late at night to try and find the energy to finish her workday. The late-night eating caused discomfort, so she would regularly go on juice cleanses for weeks at a time. Coffee and energy drinks were commonplace, which only perpetuated the sleeping and chronic cravings issues. Her lack of physical fitness and weight gain caused difficulties breathing, which would lead to a habit of chronic mouth breathing, further leading to sleep apnea and blood bio-marker changes.

Do you see the cycle? She was not broken! And neither are you! It is what is happening around you that is leading to expedited and exponential breakdown, and your body is asking for something different.

When she became aware of these normal patterns she was shocked at how much it made sense; however, she still asked the same question, "So what do I take to fix it?"

It wasn't about what she needed to take or what doctor she needed to see. It's about what habits and behaviors she needed to change.

You are the only one who can make the choice. Nobody is coming to save you. You are the knight you are waiting for, and now you can own your own health and live a life by design.

READY TO LIVE WITH OWNERSHIP?

Learn how to apply the lessons from *The Power of Ownership* and start living a life by design today.

Get FREE and exclusive access to a resource library filled with tools, videos, and ebooks that will help you experience:

- More energy
- Boosted immunity
- Better sleep
- Peak fitness
- Optimized health
- Faster recovery
- Stress resilience
- Deeper focus
- Clear purpose

Take control of your health and make it a habit, so you can BE DIFFERENT. Access the resource library now.

www.ThePowerofOwnershipBook.com/Resources

Notes

Chapter 1

1. See www.forbes.com/sites/forbescoachescouncil/2023/01/23/executive-burnout-is-real-heres-what-you-can-do-about-it/?sh=25f020a34eb1
2. See www.therecoveryvillage.com/mental-health/stress/stress-statistics/
3. See www.cdc.gov/heartdisease/facts.htm
4. See www.cdc.gov/heartdisease/facts.htm
5. See https://pubmed.ncbi.nlm.nih.gov/33309175/
6. See www.hsph.harvard.edu/obesity-prevention-source/obesity-trends-original/obesity-rates-worldwide
7. See www.americashealthrankings.org/learn/news/obesity-through-the-years
8. See www.cdc.gov/chronicdisease/resources/infographic/chronic-diseases.htm
9. See www.cdc.gov/diabetes/basics/diabetes.html#:~:text=More%20than%2037%20million%20US,death%20in%20the%20United%20States

10. See https://diabetesresearch.org/diabetes-statistics/#:~:text=Diabetes%20is%20increasing%20at%20an,to%20an%20estimated%2037.3%20million

11. See https://newsnetwork.mayoclinic.org/discussion/researchers-link-alzheimers-gene-to-type-iii-diabetes/#:~:text=Type%203%20diabetes%20occurs%20when,cognitive%20decline%20of%20Alzheimer's%20disease

12. See www.cdc.gov/aging/aginginfo/alzheimers.htm#:~:text=Younger%20people%20may%20get%20Alzheimer's,14%20million%20people%20by%202060.&text=Symptoms%20of%20the%20disease%20can,the%20risk%20increases%20with%20age

13. See https://studyfinds.org/american-families-spend-37-minutes-quality-time/

14. See www.sciencedirect.com/science/article/pii/S0022395619307381#:~:text=The%20results%20of%20this%20study,49.86%25%20from%201990%20to%202017

15. See www.cdc.gov/nchs/products/databriefs/db464.htm

16. See www.health.harvard.edu/blog/why-life-expectancy-in-the-us-is-falling-202210202835

17. See www.healthline.com/health-news/less-than-three-percent-of-americans-have-healthy-lifestyle

18. See www.ahajournals.org/doi/full/10.1161/JAHA.119.016692

19. See https://youtu.be/r3TI1d_vH84?si=-AwsA63a8uGMk31y

Chapter 2

1. See www.ncbi.nlm.nih.gov/pmc/articles/PMC5579396/
2. See www.ncbi.nlm.nih.gov/pmc/articles/PMC1959222/
3. See www.sciencedaily.com/releases/2020/03/200311100857.htm

Chapter 3

1. See www.mindtools.com/avn893g/the-holmes-and-rahe-stress-scale
2. See https://www.ncbi.nlm.nih.gov/pmc/articles/PMC5476783/
3. See https://www.who.int/data/gho/data/themes/topics/topic-details/GHO/ncd-mortality

Chapter 4

1. See https://pubmed.ncbi.nlm.nih.gov/19424767/
2. See https://www.ncbi.nlm.nih.gov/pmc/articles/PMC8716438/
3. See https://www.ncbi.nlm.nih.gov/pmc/articles/PMC6141929/#:~:text=Measuring%20Heart%20Rate%20Variability,of%20cardiovascular%20integrity%20and%20prognosis
4. See https://www.ncbi.nlm.nih.gov/pmc/articles/PMC8950456/#:~:text=High%20HRV%20is%20associated%20with,%2C%20and%20genetic%20factors%2C%20etc
5. See https://pubmed.ncbi.nlm.nih.gov/36243195/
6. See https://www.ncbi.nlm.nih.gov/pmc/articles/PMC5900369/
7. See https://www.ncbi.nlm.nih.gov/pmc/articles/PMC8950456/#:~:text=The%20HRV%20is%20influenced%20by%20many%20factors%20such%20as%20physiological,%2C%20environmental%2C%20and%20genetic%20factors
8. See https://www.whoop.com/us/en/thelocker/normal-hrv-range-age-gender/
9. See https://mspsss.org.ua/index.php/journal/article/view/532
10. See https://www.frontiersin.org/articles/10.3389/fphys.2020.566399/full

Chapter 5

1. See https://www.medicalnewstoday.com/articles/196279
2. See https://www.healthline.com/nutrition/how-much-protein-per-day
3. See https://www.ncbi.nlm.nih.gov/pmc/articles/PMC5882295/
4. See https://www.frontiersin.org/articles/10.3389/fnut.2022.955101/full
5. See https://www.spectracell.com/our-science
6. See https://www.spectracell.com/cellular-function-101
7. See https://www.cdc.gov/genomics/disease/epigenetics.htm#:~:text=Epigenetics%20is%20the%20study%20of,body%20reads%20a%20DNA%20sequence
8. See https://www.spectracell.com/blog/posts/is-methylation-good-or-bad#:~:text=Technically%2C%20methylation%20is%20neither%20inherently,(but%20not%20all)%20cases
9. See https://www.usgs.gov/special-topics/water-science-school/science/water-you-water-and-human-body
10. See https://www.ncbi.nlm.nih.gov/books/NBK555956/
11. See https://www.nhlbi.nih.gov/news/2023/good-hydration-linked-longevity
12. See https://www.nhlbi.nih.gov/news/2023/good-hydration-linked-healthy-aging
13. See https://www.pennmedicine.org/updates/blogs/health-and-wellness/2015/may/how-much-water-do-you-need-each-day#:~:text=As%20a%20general%20rule%20of,are%20performing%20non%2Dstrenuous%20activities
14. See https://www.mdpi.com/2076-3417/11/19/9093
15. See https://www.ncbi.nlm.nih.gov/books/NBK234935/
16. See https://fastlifehacks.com/the-galpin-equation/
17. See https://www.ncbi.nlm.nih.gov/pmc/articles/PMC2908954/
18. See https://www.ncbi.nlm.nih.gov/books/NBK555956/#:~:text=Some%20of%20the%20most%20common,%2C%20orthostatic%20hypotension%2C%20and%20palpitations

Chapter 6

1. See www.elon.edu/u/news/2012/05/15/professors-study-effects-of-distraction-on-exercise/
2. See www.hsph.harvard.edu/obesity-prevention-source/obesity-trends-original/obesity-rates-worldwide/#:~:text=(9)%20 A%20closer%20look%20at,are%20obese%20(36%20 percent)
3. See www.nhs.uk/live-well/exercise/exercise-health-benefits/#:~: text=It%20can%20reduce%20your%20risk,Exercise
4. See https://pubmed.ncbi.nlm.nih.gov/29293447/
5. See https://jamanetwork.com/journals/jamanetworkopen/ fullarticle/2707428
6. See www.dexafit.com/services/vo2-max-testing
7. See www.ncbi.nlm.nih.gov/pmc/articles/PMC3337929/
8. See https://news.stanford.edu/report/2021/09/15/mindsets-clearing-lens-life/
9. See https://med.stanford.edu/news/all-news/2017/03/health-care-providers-should-harness-power-of-mindsets.html

Chapter 7

1. See https://www.ncbi.nlm.nih.gov/pmc/articles/PMC377 5223/
2. See https://www.ncbi.nlm.nih.gov/books/NBK526132/
3. See https://www.healthline.com/health/how-much-deep-sleep-do-you-need#deep-sleep
4. See https://pubmed.ncbi.nlm.nih.gov/12184167/#:~:text=Sal ivation%2C%20swallowing%20rate%2C%20upper%20 esophageal,associated%20with%20faster%20gastric%20 emptying
5. See https://pubmed.ncbi.nlm.nih.gov/12395907/#:~:text= The%20gastrointestinal%20tract%20of%20vertebrate,than% 20in%20the%20pineal%20gland

6. See https://www.sleepfoundation.org/bedroom-environment/blue-light#:~:text=Blue%20light%20suppresses%20the%20body's,we%20are%20trying%20to%20sleep

7. See https://www.ncbi.nlm.nih.gov/books/NBK223808/#:~:text=The%20mean%20half%2Dlife%20of,et%20al.%2C%201989

8. See https://www.sleepfoundation.org/how-sleep-works/adenosine-and-sleep

9. See https://www.google.com/search?q=adenosine+blocker+caffiene&oq=adenosine+blocker+caffiene&aqs=chrome..69i57.5796j0j7&sourceid=chrome&ie=UTF-8

10. See https://www.ncbi.nlm.nih.gov/pmc/articles/PMC4666864/

11. See https://citeseerx.ist.psu.edu/viewdoc/download?doi=10.1.1.581.1764&rep=rep1&type=pdf

12. See https://plungejunkies.com/cold-plunge/temperatures/

13. See https://saunashare.com/sauna-cold-therapy/

14. See https://hubermanlab.com/deliberate-heat-exposure-protocols-for-health-and-performance/

15. See https://www.ncbi.nlm.nih.gov/pmc/articles/PMC3916915/

16. See https://www.goodrx.com/well-being/alternative-treatments/sauna-benefits

17. See https://pubmed.ncbi.nlm.nih.gov/8925815/

18. See https://www.verywellhealth.com/red-light-therapy-5217767

19. See https://gumc.georgetown.edu/news-release/sunlight-offers-surprise-benefit-it-energizes-infection-fighting-t-cells/

20. See https://www.ncbi.nlm.nih.gov/pmc/articles/PMC4378297/#:~:text=Grounding%20reduces%20pain%20and%20alters,chemical%20factors%20related%20to%20inflammation

21. See https://www.sciencedirect.com/science/article/pii/S2319417022001706

Chapter 8

1. See www.ncbi.nlm.nih.gov/pmc/articles/PMC8678542/
2. See www.mentalhealthfirstaid.org/2022/03/how-and-why-to-practice-self-care/
3. See www.ncbi.nlm.nih.gov/pmc/articles/PMC6119549/
4. See https://pubmed.ncbi.nlm.nih.gov/15206831/
5. See www.news10.com/news/national/study-a-10-second-hug-can-make-you-healthier-happier/

Chapter 9

1. See https://onlinelibrary.wiley.com/doi/10.1002/ejsp.674
2. See www.ncbi.nlm.nih.gov/pmc/articles/PMC3505409/#b9
3. See www.cuimc.columbia.edu/news/science-behind-behavior-change
4. See www.nia.nih.gov/news/adopting-healthy-habits-what-do-we-know-about-science-behavior-change

Acknowledgments

Alyse—your support and love is unmatched. I love you.

Mom and Dad—thank you for raising me right.

Jon Gordon and Daniel Decker—thank you for showing me the way.

The OWN IT Community—thank you for your belief and influence.

God—thank you for guiding me, preparing me, and calling me by name.

About the Author

FROM A YOUNG age, Justin Roethlingshoefer has always been self-motivated to improve, developing the discipline, habits, and ownership necessary to excel. When Justin was 13 years old, his father said, "Son, talent will get you noticed, but consistency will get you paid," and that set up his quest of redeeming the health of the world.

Over the last 20+ years Justin has worked with Stanley Cup Champions; NHL MVPs; Super Bowl Champions; Olympians; 8-, 9-, and 10-figure entrepreneurs; and Fortune 500 companies. After completing his Master's degree in Exercise Physiology with a concentration in Sports Performance, Justin sought out postgraduate research in heart rate variability, sleep, and functional medicine. He has worked as a Performance Coach in the NHL and NCAA, and founded a private camp for professional hockey players focusing on healing them from the inside out.

Through his business, keynoting, and running workshops and events, he has helped change thousands of people's lives by making the complex topic of health optimization simple and personal.

He is an Amazon best-selling author for his books: *Intent*, *Blueprint*, and *OWN IT*. They focus on peak performance, human optimization, and applying data and testing to create personalized blueprints.

Justin's knack for making the complex simple is among the best in the performance industry, and his philosophies have been adopted by Fortune 500 companies, hundreds of entrepreneurial companies, and teams in the NHL, MLB, and NFL. By taking the latest research on nutrition, training, and recovery, and packaging it into digestible, systematic, and applicable steps, Justin makes sure you can take ownership of your health and realize something different.

Index